WICCA

MOON MAGIC

A Wiccan's Guide and Grimoire for Working Magic with Lunar Energies

LISA CHAMBERLAIN

Wicca Moon Magic

Published by **Chamberlain Publications (Wicca Shorts)**

ISBN: 1539856534

ISBN-13: 978-1539856535

Disclaimer

YOUR FREE GIFT

Thank you for adding this book to your Wiccan library! To show my appreciation, I'm giving away an exclusive, free eBook to my readers—*Wicca: Little Book of Spells*.

The book is ideal for anyone looking to try their hand at practicing magic. The ten beginner-friendly spells can help you to create a positive atmosphere within your home, protect yourself from negativity, and attract love, health, and prosperity.

You can download it by visiting:

www.wiccaliving.com/bonus

I hope you enjoy it!

LEARN ABOUT WICCA
ON THE GO

Want to learn about Wicca during your morning commute, or while doing your household chores? These days it can be difficult to find the time to sit down with a good book, which is why I'm thrilled to announce that all of my books are now available in audiobook format!

Best of all, you can **get the audiobook version of this book or any other book by Lisa Chamberlain for free** as part of a 30-day Audible trial. Members receive free audiobooks every month, as well as exclusive discounts. It's a great way to experiment and see if audiobook learning works for you.

If you're not satisfied, you can cancel anytime within the trial period. You won't be charged, and you can still keep your book!

To choose your free audiobook from over 20 books about Wicca and related topics, including best-sellers *Wicca for Beginners* and *Wicca Book of Spells*, simply visit:

www.wiccaliving.com/free-audiobook

Happy Listening!

CONTENTS

INTRODUCTION

If you're reading this book, you probably already know, or at least suspect, that the Moon is magic. You may have even sought it out now and then in the clear night sky and gazed upon its majestic radiance. Perhaps you've witnessed its quiet presence in the daytime sky as well.

Many people find themselves in thrall to the silvery, mysterious energy of the Moon no matter what their spiritual or magical leanings. But for those who practice Wicca and other forms of Paganism, the Moon is a vital presence with much to teach us—about the natural rhythms of the Universe, the eternal powers of Nature, and the magical potential that is ours to tap into when we align our intentions with lunar energy.

Of course, modern practitioners of Witchcraft and magic are hardly the only people with the knowledge that the Moon is more than a giant space rock orbiting the Earth. Since the first stirrings of human civilization, the Moon has played an important role in the myths and practices of cultures around the world.

It was valued for millennia as a source of light and a way of measuring time, and like its counterpart, the Sun, it has been linked with many gods and goddesses. In both myth and magic, the Moon has been universally associated with many central concerns of human existence: love, passion, fertility, mystery, death and rebirth, and the afterlife, just to name a few.

Its magical significance was understood throughout Western Europe before the widespread domination of Christianity all but eradicated the indigenous religions of the region. Thankfully, over the last century or so, that ancient knowledge has been brought back out of the shadows, and as Wicca and other modern Pagan traditions continue to evolve and spread, more and more people are now able to take advantage of the Moon's transformational power.

This book is for anyone wanting to learn more about the connections between the Moon and the practice of magic, regardless of religious or spiritual orientation. While much of the information comes from a Wiccan perspective, and it is written to include newcomers to Wicca, the guide is not primarily focused on the Wiccan religion.

Aside from a basic overview of the Moon's role in Wiccan practice, the larger focus is on understanding the power of the Moon and its implications for an approach to magic that is aligned with lunar cycles. The practical elements are largely accessible enough for beginners, but those with more magical experience are still likely to find plenty of new ideas, concepts, and tips to enhance their practice.

So whether you follow a particular tradition of Wicca, Witchcraft, or another Pagan path, or an eclectic combination of all three—or even if you're simply just curious!—you are bound to find useful material within these pages. After all, the Moon belongs to no single religion or spiritual practice, and your connection with the Moon, and with magic itself, is uniquely your own.

In Part One, we'll examine some of the existing knowledge of the Moon in the wider "mainstream" world, including our modern scientific understanding of its relationship to the Earth as well as social and cultural observations of its effects on human beings and other animals all over the planet.

Then, we'll introduce the Wiccan perspective on the Moon, specifically in terms of the beliefs and practices surrounding this very important celestial body— the Moon's identification with the Triple Goddess, the celebration of Esbats, and the sacred act of drawing down the Moon are touched on here.

We'll also take a brief look at a related Pagan tradition of observing astrological factors that influence the Moon's energy. This initial tour sets us up for Part Two, where we'll dive into an expansive discussion of the lunar cycle.

Not many people who are new to magic have been in the habit of paying daily attention to the rhythms of the Moon's orbit around the Earth. In Part Two of this guide, we'll outline the lunar cycle in detail, charting its appearance in the sky as it moves through each phase, and explaining the key terminology used to track the Moon's progressions from one phase to the next.

We'll then lay out some systems of correspondences, used by many Witches, that align the lunar cycle with seasonal processes in Nature. These correspondences can help you gain a more intuitive sense of the Moon's energy at any particular point in the cycle, and harness that energy more effectively in your magical work. We'll also take a look at two special occasions that are optimal for lunar magic—Blue Moons and Lunar Eclipses—before moving on to the practical magic featured in Part Three.

The spells, recipes, and other hands-on information in the third and final section of this guide are all specifically related to the Moon. You'll find spellwork for each major lunar phase—New, waxing, Full, and waning—as well as workings for a Blue Moon and a Lunar Eclipse. You'll also find Tables of Correspondence for Moon-associated magical ingredients to help you create your own unique spells and rituals.

However, this lunar "Book of Shadows"—or grimoire—is just the beginning when it comes to living more magically in tune with the Moon. To that end, we also include a suggested reading list at the end of the guide, for those who wish to further pursue this fascinating aspect of Witchcraft and magic.

So enjoy your journey through these lunar pages. Once you've read this book you'll never look at the Moon the same way again!

Blessed Be.

PART ONE

THE MAGICAL MOON

NIGHT GUIDE OF THE ANCIENTS

If you live in a city, surrounded by artificial light from street lamps, buildings, and automobiles, it's very possible to live your entire existence without ever truly noticing the Moon. You may occasionally glimpse it in the night sky, but the light from the Moon will almost never be distinguishable from any other source of light.

If you live in a rural area, on the other hand, you have most likely reveled in the way the Full Moon can seem to light up everything in your environment, and you are probably more accustomed to noticing the Moon on a fairly regular basis.

But whether or not you're in the habit of observing the Moon, you and everyone else on the planet are affected, however subtly, by this mysterious satellite orbiting the Earth.

Of course, in the centuries before the advent of modern technology, everyone was definitely paying attention to the Moon. Not only was moonlight the only source of nighttime illumination other than fire, but the regular phases of the Moon's ever-shifting appearance in the sky were used to mark time.

In fact, to this day many cultures continue to follow a lunar calendar, often using it concurrently with the solar (or "Gregorian") calendar used throughout most of the world. (This is why the holidays celebrated by Jewish, Muslim, and Chinese people are on different dates each year. Even the date for the Christian holiday of Easter is determined by the Moon, falling on the Sunday following the first Full Moon after the Spring Equinox.)

It was certainly not lost on those who lived near the oceans that the Moon has an effect on the tides, and hunters all over the planet would have noted the behavioral patterns of animals based on the cycles of the Moon, and planned their hunting and fishing activities accordingly. The Moon was taken into account by agrarian cultures as well, governing the best times for planting and harvesting crops. Indeed, the Moon's importance to the survival of our ancestors was ultimately just as significant as that of the Sun.

Given the impact that this celestial body had on the daily lives of humans in ancient times, it's no surprise that the Moon figured prominently in religious practices around the globe. Indeed, Moon worship is found in the oldest religious writings of ancient Egypt, Babylonia, China and India, and deities from a wide variety of ancient cultures are associated with the Moon.

In some traditions, the Moon's ever-repeating pattern of disappearing and reappearing was associated with concepts of life, death, and rebirth. Many agricultural societies held the Moon to be a female ruler of vegetation cycles. The concept of "yin" and "yang" energies in ancient Chinese philosophy ascribed the Moon to yin, or female energy, balancing out the yang energy of the Sun.

These and other spiritual traditions from the pre-Christian world have influenced many of the beliefs and practices found within Wicca and other contemporary Pagan religions. The incorporation of lunar energies into magical work is also inspired by ancient beliefs.

But before we delve into the ways in which today's Wiccans and other Witches work with the Moon, let's take a brief look at some of what we've learned since the ancient days about this enigmatic giant rock slowly whirling around our planet.

THE 21ST-CENTURY MOON

Over the last several decades, our human relationship to the Moon has reached a whole new level, as astronauts have actually journeyed there and scientists have been learning much about the cosmos from their findings ever since.

And while we don't need a scientific understanding of the Moon to appreciate its spiritual significance to humanity or its effect on our individual lives, it's worthwhile to take a look at our celestial friend from the perspective of those who have studied it most closely.

ORIGINS AND ORBIT

The most widely accepted theory of the Moon's origins involves a collision between Earth and a giant asteroid roughly the size of Mars, which happened 4.5 billion years ago. The astral debris resulting from the crash was caught in Earth's gravitational pull, orbiting around the globe until it ultimately coalesced to form the Moon.

Another theory states that the Moon was actually a chunk of the Earth that was somehow torn from its crust and mantle and flung out into orbit.

Either scenario can help to explain why the Earth and the Moon have plenty in common beneath the surface. Although the crust of the Earth is made of rather different mineral material than the crust of the Moon, scientists have found that beneath the Earth's crust are several of the minerals that make up the bulk of the Moon's composition.

So it would seem that one way or another, the Moon and the Earth have a special connection, which you might say is symbolized by the gravitational pull that Earth has on the Moon, and the reciprocal pull that the Moon has on Earth's oceans.

The Moon's orbit around the Earth takes approximately 28 days, which is the length of a lunar month. During this orbit, the Moon's changing position relative to the Earth and the Sun causes different amounts of its surface to be illuminated, resulting in the four "phases" we identify from our perspective on Earth: **new**, **waxing**, **full**, and **waning**.

The **New Moon** occurs when the Moon is between the Earth and the Sun, so that the Sun's illumination of the Moon cannot be seen. As the Moon's movement continues, more and more of the Moon is illuminated—this is the **waxing phase**.

Once the Earth is between the Moon and the Sun, we can see a total illumination at the **Full Moon**. This illumination is then reduced again during the **waning phase**, until we once again cannot see the Moon at all.

As for the tidal effect, this is the Moon's gravity tugging on the Earth itself. The oceans on the side of Earth nearest the Moon are rising toward the Moon, while the vast waters on the other side of the globe are bulging due to the Earth's being pulled toward the Moon as well. Because the Earth is also rotating on its own axis, this high tide occurs twice a day, as does the low tide on the other end of the ever-shifting ocean.

THE BODY AND THE PSYCHE

Scientists have also observed some effects of the Moon's cycles on the behavior of animals, particularly when it comes to mating and hunting. These patterns occur both in nocturnal animals and animals primarily active during the day, and even show up in certain insects.

Furthermore, several species of birds have been seen to change their communication patterns around the Full Moon. Ocean life is also affected in the sense that high and low tides shape sea animals' behavior. Even household pets appear to be affected by the Moon, as it has been shown that cats and dogs end up in veterinary emergency rooms from accidents occurring on nights when there's a waxing or Full Moon!

Of course, humans are animals too, and as such are no less susceptible to the effects of the Moon's perpetual transformations.

It has been noted since ancient times that women's menstrual cycles tend to be in rhythm with the Moon. Ovulation and conception rates are lower at the New Moon, and tend to peak around the days leading up to, and the day of, the Full Moon. Furthermore, at least one study has shown that more births occur during times when the Moon is closest to the Earth, meaning that its gravitational pull is at its strongest.

The Moon has also been shown to affect sleep patterns, and even the outcomes of surgery—apparently, people undergoing emergency heart surgery fare better during the days around the Full Moon than during other places in the Moon's cycle.

Interestingly, what science has not been able to "prove," so far, is a phenomenon that is well-known to many who work in various human service occupations: people just seem to get a little "loony" during the Full Moon.

While no studies have confirmed that this is true, you can ask just about any bartender, child care worker, or emergency room attendant and you'll hear tales of increased accidents, erratic behavior, and downright "moodiness" during these times. In fact, the word "lunatic," rooted in the Latin word for "moon" (*luna*) comes from the belief that the changes in the Moon's appearance could cause periodic insanity.

But perhaps the biggest indicator of our awareness that the Full Moon can have a dramatic influence on humans is the archetype of the werewolf, doomed to transform from man to vicious dog every 28 days.

Generally speaking, the werewolf serves as an exaggerated and extreme symbol of the Moon's power. All the same, if you're interested enough in the Moon to be reading this book, it's highly likely you've already noticed that both the Full and the New Moon can be times of heightened sensitivity, restlessness, anxiety and/or a lack of energy, depending on how the Moon affects you personally.

For example, some people find that thinking clearly is more of a challenge around the New Moon, while others experience extreme sleepiness. It's not uncommon to feel a sense of "extra gravity" around both New and Full Moons, and intuitive types often enjoy an enhanced connection to the psychic energies swirling around in the atmosphere.

Indeed, despite how much we may have learned about the Moon on a "factual" level in the recent past, this celestial partner of the Earth still retains some very magical mysteries. This is well understood by Wiccans and other Witches, for whom the Moon is a central, sacred part of spiritual and magical practice.

We'll take a look now at some core elements of the Wiccan religion as they relate to the Moon, as well as a few other associated traditions followed by many Wiccans, Witches, and others in the contemporary Pagan world.

THE WICCAN MOON

First and foremost, the Moon is the ultimate symbol of the Goddess, the all-encompassing divine feminine in the Wiccan cosmology.

Consort to the God, whose projective, masculine energy is represented by the Sun, the Goddess embodies the receptive, feminine energy that nourishes all life. She is the night to the God's day, the Water to the God's Fire, the yin to the God's yang.

As the Moon, she appeals to the mysterious, psychic, and magical qualities within our human selves. Many Wiccans so strongly identify the Moon with the Goddess that they speak of the Moon with feminine pronouns ("she," "her") rather than the genderless "it." But regardless of the pronouns used by worshippers of the Goddess, the essence of the Moon's magical energy is always female.

Those who worship the Goddess under a specific name often identify her with a moon-associated goddess from an ancient pantheon, such as the Roman Diana, the Greek Selene, or the Celtic Rhiannon.

Others may worship her as the Egyptian Isis or Bast, even though these did not originate as Moon goddesses. Actually, the ancient Egyptians first associated the Moon with masculine deities, while the Sun's deities were often feminine. It wasn't until the cultures of ancient Egypt and Greece intermingled that Egyptian goddesses became associated with the Moon.

The Celts were also diverse about gender when it came to deities. Both the goddess Brighid and the god Lugh have solar associations, while the lunar deities include the god Oisin as well as several goddesses.

When it comes to the Moon in contemporary Wicca, however, the divine is always feminine.

THE TRIPLE GODDESS

It should be noted that in most Wiccan traditions, the Earth is also viewed as a representation of the Goddess.

Given the co-creative relationship between the Earth and the Moon, there is no inherent contradiction in this overlap—both are essential to sustaining life. However, where the Earth is typically seen as a "Mother Goddess," the Goddess of the Moon actually has three different identities, or aspects: the **Maiden**, the **Mother**, and the **Crone**.

This expanded form is the **Triple Moon Goddess**: the multifaceted deity whose diversity of roles both mirrors the cycles of the Moon—waxing, Full, and waning, and personifies the three phases of the lives of women—before, during, and after the childbearing years.

And although women experience these events in a linear sequence, their lives are also part of a cycle, because Wiccans believe in reincarnation. After the death of the Crone comes rebirth, and the new journey leading back to the realm of the Maiden.

While the concepts surrounding the Triple Moon Goddess (also known simply as the **Triple Goddess**) largely originate with the work of spiritualists in the mid-1900s, there is precedent for a three-fold feminine deity in ancient written and pictorial artifacts.

Among Wiccans, two well-known goddesses with triple associations are the Celtic Brighid, goddess of healing, poetry, and smithcraft; and the Greek Hera, who appears in some myths in three different roles: Girl, Woman, and Widow. Neither was particularly associated with the Moon in ancient times, but there are some links between three separate Moon goddesses who form a kind of trinity, such as Artemis, Selene and Hecate.

Many Wiccans worship the Triple Moon Goddess in a similar fashion, whether they are all from the same ancient pantheon or "borrowed" from different cultural groups. For example, she may be Rhiannon in the Maiden aspect, the Greek Demeter as the Mother, and Hecate as the Crone. These designations are based on the characteristics of the goddesses and their roles as they appear in their native mythologies, and are not generally interchangeable.

Furthermore, each goddess has her own magical domains, also rooted in original mythology, and so can be called upon for assistance with related magical goals. These correspondences are linked to both her identity and her archetypal role.

If you're interested in learning more about working magic with any aspect of the Triple Goddess, it's worth reading the rich mythology surrounding these ancient deities and exploring connections with any you feel intuitively drawn to.

Like the individual goddesses who represent them, each aspect of the Triple Goddess has her own archetypal identity. Each symbolizes various elements in Nature, including animal and plant life, seasons and times of day, and different characteristics of the human experience.

Although the emphasis is on the feminine, each of the associations within the domain of the Triple Goddess is relevant to both males and females, since all of us contain both masculine and feminine energies within our psyches.

Likewise, we all experience our own cycles of birth, maturation and death over the course of our lives, whether it be in regard to our relationships, projects, ambitions, etc. In one way or another, we all resonate with all three aspects of the Triple Goddess at various points in our personal journeys.

Let's briefly meet the Maiden, Mother, and Crone as they exist in the Wiccan cosmology. Then in Part Two, we'll take a closer look at the phases of the Moon they represent, including the many different possibilities for magic that are supported by these lunar rhythms.

THE MAIDEN

The Maiden aspect of the Triple Goddess emerges with the crescent Moon, and reigns during the waxing days as the Moon grows toward Full.

She represents the youth and innocence of life before motherhood, and so is associated with all things "new": the dawn, the sunrise, the Spring, young animals, and all that is ripening into fullness.

The Maiden assists with activities involving creativity, beauty, exploration, self-discovery and self-expression.

She supports the characteristics of self-confidence, intelligence and independence.

Goddesses who typically represent the Maiden include the Greek goddesses Persephone and Artemis, the Celtic Rhiannon, and the Nordic Freya, and many others from around the globe.

THE MOTHER

The Mother Goddess is aligned with the days just before, during and after the Full Moon.

Having matured from Maiden to Mother, her time is the afternoon, when the day's light is at its strongest, and her season is the lush full swing of Summer.

As the one who brings forth new life, she is the goddess most associated with manifestation of all kinds, as well as adulthood, responsibility, and tending and nurturing what has come into being.

As the symbol of the Full Moon, she is often revered as the most powerful of the three aspects of the Triple Goddess.

The Mother is often worshipped in the guise of the Roman Ceres, the Greek Demeter and Selene, and the Celtic Badb and Danu, among others.

THE CRONE

As the Moon wanes, becoming less and less visible with each passing day, the Crone steps into her power.

The most mysterious of the three aspects, she is associated with sunset and night, and Autumn and Winter—the darkest times in the cycle of life and death on Earth.

Finished now with the duties of motherhood, the Goddess turns her focus to the domains of death and ultimate rebirth. Her understanding of these cycles makes her the wise elder, and she supports experiences involving aging, completions, prophecies and visions, transformation, and death—both literal and figurative.

The Crone reigns during the dark of the Moon, patiently tending the nights until the New Moon returns.

She is represented by a wide cultural range of goddesses, including the Russian Baba Yaga, the Greek Hecate, and the Celtic Morrigan and Cailleach Bear.

THE ESBATS

While every aspect of the Triple Goddess—and corresponding Moon phase—is sacred to Wiccans, the divine feminine is particularly honored at every Full Moon.

These celebrations are called **Esbats**, and occur either 12 or 13 times per calendar year, depending on how the lunar calendar lines up with the solar (or "Gregorian") calendar. While the God is honored at the Sabbats—the four solar holidays and four cross-quarter days that make up the Wheel of the Year—the Esbats belong to the Goddess.

Some Wiccans call the Esbats the "second Wheel of the Year," but this doesn't mean that Full Moon celebrations are less important than the Sabbats. Wicca is rooted in gender polarity—the Universe being made up of both male and female energies in equal parts—and so the lunar/Esbat cycle is every bit as central as the solar/Sabbat cycle.

The details and particular focus of the Esbat rituals vary widely among covens and solitary Wiccans. Very often, the focus of the rituals will align with the time of year, and/or honoring a specific aspect of the Goddess. For example, an Esbat taking place in late Autumn may be devoted to a Crone goddess such as Kali (Hindu) or Badb (Celtic), while a Spring Esbat might focus on Maiden goddesses like Diana (Greek) or Ostara (Saxon).

Many covens and informal circles will work magic together, since the Moon's power is particularly strong on these occasions. Magical goals include individual intentions as well as communal and even global needs, such as healing, abundance, and respect for the Earth and her natural resources.

Just as each solar Sabbat celebrates a distinct point along the Wheel—such as the height of Summer at Litha/Solstice or the beginning of the harvest season at Lammas/Lughnasa—each Full Moon has its own distinct energy. For example, the Full Moons of late Summer and Autumn tend to have a more electric feeling than the quiet, more subtle energies of Winter Moons.

Each Full Moon also has its own name, which generally honors an aspect of the natural world, agricultural cycles, animal behavior, and even human activities. There are several names for each Moon, which are borrowed from various Native American traditions, as well as the ancient Celts and, more rarely, Chinese traditions. For example, the Full Moon in January may be known as the Ice Moon, the Wolf Moon, or the Stay Home Moon.

The most commonly used names in Wiccan traditions are the following:

Month	Moon Name
January	Cold Moon (also Hunger)
February	Quickening Moon (also Snow)
March	Storm Moon (also Sap)
April	Wind Moon (also Pink)
May	Flower Moon (also Milk)
June	Sun Moon (also Strong Sun and Rose)
July	Blessing Moon (also Thunder)
August	Corn Moon (also Grain)
September	Harvest Moon
October	Blood Moon
November	Mourning Moon (also Frost)
December	Long Nights Moon

It's important to note that not every coven meets at the Full Moon to hold their Esbats. Some choose to celebrate at the New Moon instead, while others will strive to observe both points on the "second Wheel."

Solitary Witches often observe both New and Full Moons as well, and may also honor the Half Moons with at least a small ritual or candle-lighting.

In the general sense of the word, "Esbat" really refers to any ritual that honors the Moon and the Goddess.

DRAWING DOWN THE MOON

One very highly significant ritual that takes place at every Full Moon Esbat is the act of drawing down the Moon. This is a transformative process that brings the energy of the Moon—and therefore, the energy of the Goddess—into the physical body of the Witch.

In a coven ceremony, the High Priestess will perform the act, usually with words of invocation, and become the human embodiment of the Goddess on behalf of the group. Depending on the tradition followed by the coven, this can be an elaborate ritual with many spoken elements, gestures, and the use of symbolic ritual tools, or it may be fairly simple, yet elegant.

The same is true for solitary Wiccans who make drawing down the Moon part of their practice—while many follow older, more established traditions, many more approach drawing down the Moon in a more individualized manner. They may use the athame, or ritual knife, to symbolically draw the Moon's power into their bodies, or they may simply stand silently under the Moon with their palms turned upward.

This sacred ritual creates a powerful experience for the participant, who may feel strong physical or emotional sensations after connecting with the Goddess in this way, and it's a unique experience for every individual.

Ideally, drawing down the Moon takes place at the exact moment that the Moon becomes Full. If this isn't possible, Wiccans will try to hold the ritual as closely as possible to that moment, which is typically the night before.

Standing outside directly under the Moon is considered to be the most powerful location for this work, but standing indoors at a window and/or with a candle dedicated to the Goddess is also effective.

Strictly speaking, drawing down the Moon is a Full Moon ritual, but some eclectic Wiccans incorporate it into their practice at other times during the lunar cycle as well. In every instance, the energy harnessed from this connection with the Goddess is used to charge the ensuing ritual activities, including any magical work undertaken at this time.

THE WITCH, THE MOON, AND THE STARS

While the specific practices described above originate with traditional Wicca, working with the feminine power of the Moon is not exclusive to this spiritual path.

Many who identify as Witches but not Wiccans, and plenty of those who identify with the more general term Pagan, also honor and connect with the Moon at various times throughout the lunar cycle. Their ways of doing so are quite diverse, and many eclectic types create their own rituals and practices, rather than following established traditions.

For example, a Witch whose practice is steeped in herbal knowledge and gardening might choose to plant seeds at the New Moon in order to honor the new life that this phase represents. In lieu of a formal ritual, a group of like-minded Witches and other Pagans might simply hold a potluck feast at the Full Moon. Non-Wiccans may or may not worship the divine feminine in the form of a deity, though many do revere the Goddess and/or ancient goddesses associated with the Moon.

Furthermore, many Wiccans and non-Wiccans alike take astrological circumstances into account when working with the Full Moon, in addition to (or instead of) focusing on seasonal influences or aspects of the Goddess. Some traditions identify the current Sun sign and name the Moon accordingly, rather than using one of the more traditional names explained above. The ritual and magic surrounding this Full Moon are centered on the attributes of the Zodiac sign.

For example, the Full Moon that occurs between October 23 and November 21 is called the Scorpio Moon. This is a time to reflect on the nature of illusion and to engage in piercing through illusions that are blocking our progress in some way. Magic at this time may be worked for protection from negativity, enhanced intuition, or deeper connection with one's inner power.

Alternatively, some Witches work according to the sign the Moon is in, so that the Full Moon occurring between the dates given above would be called the Taurus Moon. The Moon is always in the opposite sign from the Sun when it's Full, so this is fairly easy to pinpoint once you're familiar with the Zodiac wheel.

Given this lunar relationship between the opposite signs, some traditions actually incorporate both signs (e.g. Scorpio and Taurus) into their Full Moon rituals, for a balanced approach to tuning into the energies of this powerful phase in the cycle.

Astrological considerations don't only apply to the Full Moon, however. The Moon spends approximately two and a half days in each sign during its orbit around the Earth, and those who are attuned to these subtle shifts will notice certain patterns in circumstances and behavior that correspond to each sign.

For example, when the Moon is in Aries, people tend to feel more assertive and even argumentative, and events may unfold rapidly and then come to an equally quick end.

Astrological information can be used to guide magical work as well. In the case of Aries, which is located at the beginning of the Zodiac, spells involving beginnings are favored.

When the Moon is en route from one sign to the next, it is considered to be "void of course." Many Wiccans and other Witches recommend abstaining from spellwork at this time, as the lunar energies are "on break," so to speak, and magic is likely to have little effect. These "void" periods are just a few hours long on average, but occasionally last for a day or more.

Those who are really into astrology might also take into account the Moon's position in relation to the planets, particularly when an alignment with one or more planets has a significant energetic effect on events, emotions, and other circumstances. However, this is more advanced knowledge than most people find necessary, at least when it comes to ritual and magic.

Too much detail can definitely end up distracting one's focus in this regard. There's really no need to become an astrology buff in order to work with the Moon's magical energy. If you feel called to learn more and incorporate the planets and the stars into your relationship with the Moon, go for it. If not, that's perfectly fine, too.

DIVING DEEPER

Since the beginning of human history, the Moon has figured into our daily lives in one way or another, even if most people living in today's Western mainstream culture no longer realize it. Various cultures around the world continue to recognize, appreciate, and celebrate the Moon's power, with a wide range of traditions and practices for harnessing this special energy for magic.

Here, we have briefly examined the main elements of the Moon's role in the core beliefs and practices of Wicca, as well as a few related practices that incorporate older astrological traditions. Next, we'll take a closer look at the mysterious power of lunar energy and a much more comprehensive view of the lunar cycle.

You'll find a detailed breakdown of each phase of the cycle, including the ever-changing appearance of the Moon in the sky as it orbits the Earth and the magical associations of each phase. From New to Full, to Dark and back to New again, the never-ending cycle of the Moon presents a rich variety of opportunities to tune into the energies of the natural world and enhance your spellwork.

Indeed, the potential for Moon magic goes far beyond working spells under the Full Moon, as we will see in the discussion of each lunar phase. We'll look at relationships between the lunar cycle and the Wheel of the Year, as well as growth cycles as observed in wild and cultivated plant life.

These correspondences can help you deepen your magical practice on a profound level as you tune in to the connections between your own life and the ever-shifting tides of waxing and waning, attracting and releasing, growing and dying back. Adopting a practice of living in rhythm with the Moon can open up amazing pathways to a deeper connection with the Universe, and enhance your quality of life.

Finally, there are two aspects of the Moon's relationship with magic that have not been discussed in this initial overview: Blue Moons and Lunar Eclipses. These special events are observed and honored by Wiccans, Witches, and other Pagans, and are often even noted in the mainstream world.

The rare energy of Blue Moons and the highly charged energy of Eclipses can enhance magic like no other force on Earth or in the cosmos, and the opportunities they present should not be missed. However, it's more useful to examine these phenomena once the lunar cycle is more fully understood.

So let's dive deeper now into the magical waters of the Moon.

PART TWO

RHYTHMS OF THE MOON

LUNAR ENERGY AND MAGIC

Have you ever heard the saying, "it must be the Moon?"

Usually used in a joking manner to explain away any strange events or bizarre behavior witnessed when the Moon is Full, this phrase has much more truth to it than most people would believe.

Mainstream culture tends to laugh off the notion of Moon-influenced feelings and behavior, but, as we saw in Part One, the Moon does have effects on people and animals. This tends to be most obvious during the days surrounding the Full Moon, whether we're noticing unusual behavior in our pets or children, or feeling ourselves to be abnormally "moody."

But while you may already be aware that the "Full Moon effect" is not a myth, you may not realize that *all* phases of the Moon's cycle influence us on some level, however subtle it may be for those who aren't yet attuned to lunar energy.

Just as the Earth has its own energy, which is independent from the energy it receives from the Sun, the Moon, too, emits an energy that is subtle, yet distinctive. Unlike the Sun's masculine, projective energy, lunar energy is feminine and receptive. This is the energy of the Goddess.

This power has often been described as magnetic, which makes sense to anyone who has literally felt "pulled" in some way by the Moon. Some particularly sensitive people actually feel a physical tug in their bodies at the Full or New Moon, while others just notice a heightened sense of awareness to everything in their environment.

The way you personally respond to the Moon's energy will depend on many factors, including diet and exercise patterns, as well as influences in your astrological birth chart. Indeed, everyone's relationship with the Moon's cycle is unique, but if you start paying close attention to how you think and feel during each phase, you'll be better able to understand how these rhythms affect your personal power. Then you can use these discoveries to strengthen your magical abilities.

What does the Moon's energy have to do with magic? As multi-sensory beings, we are constantly interacting with unseen energies coming from every direction—from other people, from media, from the food we eat and the buildings we spend our days and nights in. Everything we interact with has an effect on our personal energetic makeup.

We tend to focus on what we experience through our five physical senses—sight, sound, touch, taste, and smell. But our sixth sense—intuition—is the most crucial mode of perception when it comes to magic. And the energy of the Moon is tailor-made for interacting with the energy of our intuition, which is also feminine, receptive, and magnetic in nature.

So when we consciously connect with lunar energy, we are opening up our own capacity to channel that energy into drawing what we desire to us, and releasing what we don't want from our lives. And when we do so in conscious harmony with the energetic rhythms of the Moon's cycle, we can truly amplify the power of our magical work.

TRACKING THE MOON

Before considering the relationship between the Moon and magic, however, it's important to identify the phases of the lunar cycle in more detail. After all, you can't truly take advantage of the opportunities that lunar energies present if you don't know what's happening in the sky when you're casting your spells!

Let's take a look now at two different frameworks for describing and tracking the movement of the Moon as it orbits the Earth, and then we'll discuss the magical opportunities that each phase presents.

LIGHT AND SHADOW

In the first framework, the Moon's cycle is tracked by its appearance in the sky.

It begins as a barely-detectable sliver at the New Moon. Over the next few days, the sliver becomes larger and more defined, almost resembling the tip of a fingernail—this is called the Crescent Moon. From here, the Moon continues to grow—or "wax"— on its way to becoming Full. At the mid-point between New and Full, we see the waxing Half Moon, with the illuminated half on the right and the shadowed half on the left.

As the circle begins to be filled out with light, it becomes "gibbous," a word used in astronomy to describe the bulging appearance of the Moon during the days just before and after it's completely Full. Finally, when the circle is completely lit, we are looking at the Full Moon.

In the days just after the Full point, the Moon is gibbous again, then continues to shrink—or "wane"—further back to Half. This time, the light half is on the left, with the shadowed half on the right.

More and more of the Moon is covered in shadow as it wanes back to its Crescent point, and then completely disappears. This window of time before it is visible again is the Dark Moon. Once the sliver returns, the cycle begins again.

MEASURING TIME

The other way of tracking the Moon's cycle is to divide it into four quarters, spread out over roughly 28 days. Each quarter lasts approximately seven days, adding up to create what we call the lunar "month."

The first quarter begins at the New Moon and ends at the waxing Half. The second quarter runs from there until the Full Moon. The third quarter begins immediately after the Moon turns Full and lasts until the waning Half Moon, and the fourth quarter closes out the cycle through the Dark Moon, ending just as the Moon reemerges into New.

It's interesting to note that while the two systems are not technically in conflict with each other, in terms of covering the full lunar cycle, there is something of an asymmetrical "glitch" when you try to align them. The ordered, even-numbered quarter system contains 4 units, which doesn't quite align with the 5 major marking points—New, Half, Full, Half, Dark—of the older, somewhat looser framework.

This is because the quarter system doesn't actually take the Dark Moon period into account. In reality, the Moon takes 29.5 days to complete its orbit, which is a number that 4 doesn't divide into equally, so there's a slight "lag" during the Dark time between the fourth and first quarters.

Furthermore, the period of amplified energetic influence that the Full Moon exerts is much longer than the brief period of time when it's fully illuminated. In the Witching world, the Full moon phase is actually considered to be 5 days long—from the two days before Full, when the Moon is still gibbous, until two days after, when the waning is just becoming visible.

Some people go even further, designating a full week to the Full Moon. But for the purposes of working with lunar energies, it can be argued that the Full Moon phase begins and ends when you *feel* it beginning and ending. To some extent, the entire lunar cycle is a bit like that. Remember, it's ultimately about your personal intuitive perception—your sixth sense.

Nonetheless, the quarter system may be more appealing to some, as it can be easier to keep track of. In fact, many calendars note the beginning mark of each quarter. And it's particularly helpful when you don't have the opportunity to go looking at the Moon every single night. (In fact, depending on where it is in its orbit and your own sleep schedule, you may not be able to see it at night.)

The truth is, it really doesn't matter how you track the phases, as long as you're at least aware of when the New and Full Moons occur—these are, after all, the two most energetically powerful times of the cycle.

So if you're new to paying close attention to the Moon, start by paying attention to these two points. As you get into the habit of "tracking the Moon" in this way, you'll find yourself attuning to the more subtle, continuous rhythms of the various energies of the Moon's complete cycle. You'll also get a better feel for timing your magic to align as closely as possible with each lunar phase.

Now that the full cycle has been more specifically illuminated, let's delve into the magical implications for working in harmony with the rhythms of the Moon.

MAGICAL TIMING AND THE LUNAR CYCLE

Generally speaking, the relationship between magic and the Moon can be summed up as follows: as the Moon grows, we work magic for increase; as it wanes, we work magic for decrease.

Another way to say it is that when you're seeking to bring something into your life, you work with the waxing Moon, and when you want to banish or release some unwanted element of your life, you work during the waning phase.

The transitional point between these two opposites is the Full Moon, a time of "harvest" as we celebrate what we have manifested over the first half of the cycle. We then essentially "clean up" afterward, identifying and releasing what is no longer needed throughout the second half of the cycle. At the New Moon, we set new intentions for the next cycle of manifestation, and on and on it goes.

The rhythm of this cycle can be visualized as the rhythm of the tides, which the Moon, of course, is causing. The waves grow bigger and come closer, covering more of the shoreline as the tide rises. The incoming surf peaks at high tide, and then recedes, exposing more and more shoreline until it reaches the low tide mark, and begins to rise again.

This is the basic framework, and yet there's much more to it than the simple dichotomy of "wax/wane," "flow, ebb," or "increase/decrease." Many Witches deepen their practice of working with the Moon by incorporating more complex systems of alignments and associations within the lunar cycle.

For starters, as we saw in Part One, those who worship the Triple Goddess will generally call upon the appropriate aspect when working magic aligned with the Moon—the Maiden is asked for assistance in the waxing phase, the Mother at the Full Moon, and the Crone when the Moon is on the wane.

Others may observe additional correspondences between the phases of the lunar cycle and the seasons, the Sabbats on the Wheel of the Year, and/or the growing cycles of plant life, which is the basis for so much of the symbolism inherent to Wicca and other forms of the Craft.

These systems can provide beautiful ways of further attuning to the Moon's subtle rhythms, as we will see next.

SEASONS AND SABBATS

Although it's the Earth's orbit around the Sun that is responsible for the turning of the seasons, the ever-shifting appearance of the Moon in the sky can be seen as a mirroring of the same cycle.

For example, Spring is the time of new life and increasing growth, which corresponds to the Moon's waxing phase. The Full Moon represents Summer, with its explosion of vegetation and the flourishing of young animal life, while the Autumn corresponds with the waning phase, as plants die back and animals prepare for the end of the warmer seasons. The Winter, then, is represented by the Dark Moon, as all life waits for the cycle to begin again.

This system of seasonal alignments can enhance our understanding of the subtle distinctions between the various magical aims that are most appropriate at different points in the lunar cycle.

However, it's rather unevenly distributed in terms of the actual length of seasons—after all, Summer and Winter are just as long as Spring and Autumn, so in a sense it's disproportionate to grant them only a few days of the Moon's cycle while the other seasons get nearly two weeks.

But if you're willing to expand the framework and go deeper into the Wheel of the Year, you'll find that there's a much more evenly-spaced system that truly illuminates the alignment between the patterns of the Sun and the Moon.

Using the eight Sabbats as a "map" of the Moon's travels, we can view the incremental shifts of the waxing and waning phases more closely, allowing for the "in-between" seasons to guide us into even more optimal timing of our magical efforts.

One way to do this is to match the Moon's quarter marks with the solar Sabbats. For example, the Full Moon can be represented by the Summer Solstice (also known in Wicca as Litha) and the New Moon by the Winter Solstice (or, Yule).

This would place each Half Moon at an equinox point—the waxing Half at Spring (Ostara) and the waning Half at Autumn (Mabon)—with the crescent and gibbous phases represented by the four Earth Sabbats: Imbolc, Beltane, Lughnasa and Samhain.

Then the days between Samhain and Yule, when the nights are the longest that they'll be all year, belong to the Dark Moon.

(Of course, if you live in the Southern Hemisphere, these correspondences run in reverse—or counter-clockwise—with Yule being the Summer Solstice and therefore the time of the Full Moon, and the New Moon aligning with Litha, and so on.)

This system of Sabbat alignments works well for many Witches, but for those who live in northern climates with cold, long winters, it doesn't *quite* line up exactly with how the seasons are experienced. In these regions, the New Moon, as a symbol of the end of darkness and the beginning of new life, is actually more closely aligned with Imbolc, which is the Sabbat celebrating the first stirrings of Spring.

Therefore, many Witches align the Moon's quarter marks with the Earth-based Sabbats instead. This shifts the system by a half-season, but still represents the overall timing and feel of the changes in the climate and landscape where they live.

In this framework, the Full Moon aligns with the cross-quarter day of Lughnasa (also Lammas), which is the first of the three harvest festivals. Given that "harvest" is a theme of the Full Moon, this makes as much sense as pairing the Full Moon with the Summer Solstice.

Furthermore, the Dark Moon period then falls between Yule and Imbolc—from late December through the end of January, when many start to feel as if the Winter will never end!

Depending on where you live, one of these alignment systems may make more intuitive sense than the other. Those who live near the equator, for example, may prefer the solar alignments, since the changes in seasons are not as noticeable as they are in the regions closer to the North and South poles.

For the purposes of this guide, however, we will use the Earth-based alignments as shown in the following table, since they more accurately reflect the seasons in the regions where Western Witchcraft originated.

Moon Phase	Sabbat	Season
New	Imbolc (Feb 2)	Late Winter / Early Spring
Waxing Crescent	Spring Equinox (Ostara)	Spring
Waxing Half	Beltane (May 1)	Late Spring / Early Summer
Half to Full (Gibbous)	Summer Solstice (Litha)	Summer
Full	Lughnasa / Lammas (Aug 1)	Late Summer / Early Autumn
Full to Half (Gibbous)	Autumn Equinox (Mabon)	Autumn
Waning Half	Samhain (Oct 31)	Late Autumn / Early Winter
Waning Crescent	Winter Solstice (Yule)	Winter
Dark	(none)	(period between Yule and Imbolc)

So how do these correspondences between Moon phases and the Sabbats and seasons affect magical work? Depending on how you approach your own magical practice, there are a number of possibilities.

You might, for example, use them to choose an auspicious timing for a particular spell. If you're seeking to draw romantic love into your life—or to reenergize an existing relationship—

you know that the waxing phase is the best time to work. This gives you a window of two weeks.

But what if you want to narrow it down further? Take a look at the Sabbat correspondences and you'll notice that Beltane, a Sabbat associated with love and lust, falls at the waxing Half Moon. Why not choose this date, drawing on the bright, playful energies of Beltane as you send your magical intention for love out into the Universe?

Of course, many Wiccans make use of correspondences between magical purposes and the days of the week. In this system, Friday is the most ideal for working love spells, which may or may not line up with the waxing Half Moon.

If the waxing Half does fall on a Friday, then you're looking at a truly stellar alignment for your particular goal! If it falls on a different day, then you will need to use your intuition to decide on the best timing for your love spell. As always when it comes to magic, do what works best for you.

Another approach is to simply incorporate the *feeling* of the corresponding season into your magical work. For example, in a spell for love you can imagine the delicious warming up of late Spring / early Summer—that promising preview of the warmth and lushness of Summer coming into full swing—and use the feelings created by those thoughts to fuel your magic.

And if you're the type to create your own spells from scratch, you can use the corresponding season and/or Sabbat as inspiration for deciding on ingredients. For example, there are tons of herbs associated with romantic love, but which ones are at their peak during the Beltane season? Which are commonly used at Beltane celebrations?

Doubling up on your correspondences in this way can make your magic incredibly potent!

ALIGNING WITH GROWTH CYCLES

Another creative framework for magical correspondences aligns the phases of the Moon with the stages of the life cycle of plants.

Although there is obviously a lot of variation between different kinds of plants—flowers, shrubs, trees, herbs, wild vs. cultivated plant life, etc.—a basic pattern is observed in the workings of the world of vegetation.

With a few exceptions (like mosses, ferns and mushrooms), every plant begins as a seed. Given the right conditions of soil, water and light, the seed will root and begin to grow. As it reaches upward toward the sun, leaves begin to develop, followed by buds which become flowers. The flowers are pollinated—by bees, moths, butterflies, bats, or wind, depending on the species—which produces the fruit of the plant. The fruit contains the seeds that will start the next cycle of growth.

(Note that the term "fruit" is being loosely applied here, and doesn't necessarily refer to something we would eat. A pinecone, for example, contains the seeds needed to grow new pine trees. Nuts are also considered fruits in this growth cycle model.)

Once the fruit has reached its ripest point, it will either be eaten by an animal or drop to the ground. Either way, the seeds will ultimately find their way back into the soil, beginning the cycle all over again.

When we view the growth cycle and the lunar cycle together, we can align the two quite symmetrically, like this:

Moon Phase	Growth Cycle Phase
New	Seed
Waxing Crescent	Root
Waxing Half	Leaf
Half to Full (Gibbous)	Bud
Full	Flower
Full to Half (Gibbous)	Fruit
Waning Half	Harvest
Waning Crescent	Compost
Dark	(Rest)

How are these correspondences meaningful to magic? Aside from providing us with another framework for viewing the phases of the Moon, the life cycle of plants serves as a great metaphor for the co-creative nature of magical manifestation.

Too often, beginning practitioners of magic will work spells for big goals and then sit around wondering why they didn't meet the partner of their dreams or become a millionaire this week. For one thing, the Law of Attraction—which is a big part of magic—states that you get what you think about, so if you're constantly focusing on how you still haven't seen your dream come true, that's exactly what you'll continue to experience.

It's important to direct your thoughts to the manifestation *itself*, not the lack of it. More to the point, however, is the need to do your part in the co-creation of what you seek to manifest.

If you learn to think of yourself as a magical "gardener," you will get a clearer sense of how and why your participation is a key component.

Whether we intend to grow flowers, herbs, vegetables, or trees, there is a balance between the actions we need to take, and the transformative processes that Nature alone is responsible for. We do the planting, the watering and nurturing, but the creation of leaf, bud, flower and fruit is all Nature's doing.

When our manifestation has fully culminated, it's up to us to either reap the fruit or let it over-ripen and drop to the ground. The composting remains of whatever we don't use are naturally designed to propagate new life the following season, but we can give this process great assistance and direction by tending the soil, weeding out what is unwanted, and preparing the garden for its winter rest.

Furthermore, the growth cycle illustrates the role of *timing* in magic, not only as it relates to the energies of Moon phases, but also in terms of how manifestation actually occurs as it moves from the invisible plane to the physical plane. Just as each stage of the growth cycle has its particular purpose in the overall enterprise of plant creation, magical manifestation happens in stages.

Most often, the initial developments taking place are not visible to the eye, just as a seed takes root under the surface of the soil. And even as the manifestation begins to emerge, it may not immediately be recognized for what it is, just as most seedlings tend to resemble each other, no matter what species of plant they are. For those with untrained eyes, it takes some time before they've grown enough to be distinguishable from other plants.

The beginnings of our manifestations can be like this—a chance conversation with an acquaintance that turns out to be a tip on a new job possibility, or a run of what *seems* to be bad luck (a fender bender, a delayed flight) that puts us in the path of our next true love. Most realized goals can be traced back to a winding chain of actions and events that seemed unrelated or insignificant until the manifestation became clear.

So if your magic is to succeed, it's not enough to simply plant a seed of intention. You'll need to nurture it. You'll need to be willing to leave your house, get out and meet people, and yes, maybe even buy a lottery ticket (though if you're convinced that your only chance at wealth is through a game with incredibly stiff odds, you won't be open to other, unseen possibilities).

You'll also need to practice being alert to subtle nudges from the Universe—i.e., your intuition—that may be trying to show you the seedlings of your intentions poking up through the soil.

Finally, you'll have to have patience, since no matter what actions you take, Nature works on its own schedule.

Be aware of the difference between what you can do and what is strictly up to the Universe, and be willing to let the manifestation unfold according to divine timing. Of course, it's true that some manifestations *do* happen very quickly, just as some plants literally do spring up overnight. But even these still started out as tiny seeds, hidden from view.

PUTTING IT ALL TOGETHER: THE LUNAR PHASES

As you can see, there are many ways to view the Moon's cycle when it comes to magic.

It begins with the understanding of waxing and waning energies, which correspond to the rising and ebbing tides. Adding the seasons and Sabbats to this framework integrates the magical energies of the Wheel of the Year into the lunar cycle. The Earth energy is further intensified by the growth cycle alignments, providing a microcosm, or inner "wheel," of connection with Nature.

Of course, not everyone will resonate with these approaches, as everyone's magical practice is unique and personal to them. However, those who do incorporate two or more of these systems of correspondence find that they come to a far more intuitive relationship with the process of manifestation than they had before.

Now we'll take a deeper look at the lunar cycle, with an eye for how the energies of each phase can help you shape your magic. We'll examine how each of the seasonal and growth cycle alignments can inform your choices in terms of goals to work for, and how you approach your spellwork.

For those who work with aspects of the Goddess, individual deities particularly suited for each particular Moon phase are also included, though please note that these are just a few examples, and that there is plenty of room for overlap between adjacent phases. In other words, goddesses who align with the waxing Crescent Moon are also suitable for other phases of the waxing half of the cycle, etc.

Utilizing these correspondence systems to help structure your magical practice will definitely enhance your spellwork, but it can also help you zero in on the goals that are most likely to be achieved at any given time. This is very helpful during those times when you want to set intentions for everything under the Sun and don't know where to start!

The discussion below outlines a trajectory of sorts for the manifestation process. However, it's important to note here that many, if not most magical goals are realized over a longer stretch of time than just one lunar cycle—especially large and significant ones.

For example, if you're intending to start a family, you're obviously not going to give birth to a child in two weeks' time. Likewise, it would very rarely be a good idea to get married at the Full Moon to someone you just met at the waxing Half-Moon!

However, many simple, short-term goals can be realized in one lunar cycle, and many long-term goals see increments of progress during these times. And you can learn to see the work of the waning phase—releasing what isn't wanted or no longer serves you—as part of the process of manifesting what you do want, as we will see below.

But regardless of how any given magical intention turns out, if you make a practice of working according to lunar rhythms, you will be strengthening your sixth-sense connection to the Universal energies, and enhancing your magic as a result.

NEW MOON

The New Moon marks the very earliest beginnings of the lunar cycle. After a period of darkness, with no source of light in the night sky, the tiniest sliver of the Moon's surface emerges. It's not yet big enough to be visible to the naked eye, but it can still be felt, energetically, by many who are attuned to lunar rhythms.

Just as Imbolc marks the first stirrings of new life beneath the still-cold ground, the New Moon extends a promise of new things to come. This is the seed-time of the growth cycle—all the potential of a new manifestation is still contained within a small packet of highly charged energy, invisible to us as it remains buried in the soil.

This is a good time for dreaming of what you wish to create in your life. Perhaps you don't know exactly what you want it to look like, but taking some time to imagine how you will feel once it has manifested will guide you toward a more specific vision as the month goes on.

For example, if you want to get a new job, but don't have a clear sense of where or in what field you'd like to work, use the New Moon as a time to open up to various possibilities—including those you haven't consciously thought of—and tune in to your intuition about which ones feel the most alive to you. Work a spell that asks for help in clarifying your employment goals, or invite a number of potential offers to come your way so you can make decisions from a highly empowered place.

Traditionally, magic aimed at initiating new projects and ventures is favored at this time, but anything involving attracting or increasing what you desire is appropriate here. It's also a good time for formalizing any intentions aimed at self-improvement, whether it be an exercise plan or a resolution to learn more about a particular topic.

It's helpful to keep in mind that New Moon spells aren't really about *instant* manifestation. They're about new beginnings, initiating actions that will bear fruit down the road. We plant the seeds, water them gently, and remain patient as they begin to germinate.

Many Witches work their spells as close as possible to the exact time of the New Moon, or just after, as this is thought to be the most potent time to harness the magical energies of this phase. Others prefer to cast New Moon spells during daylight hours, since at this point in the cycle the Moon rises and sets with the Sun.

Of course, you may not have the luxury of following either of these strategies, depending on your daily schedule. If this is the case, don't let it worry you. Just do your best to work on the actual day (or night) of the New Moon or no more than one day after, if you want to align your work with these particular energies, which will continue to influence events throughout the waxing phase.

Goddesses: Diana (Roman), Artemis (Greek), Astarte (Phoenician)

WAXING CRESCENT

Beginning with the day after the New Moon, and over the next few days, the Crescent Moon becomes more and more noticeable in the sky. The dream-time is turning more outwardly toward manifestation as the seedlings we have planted start taking root in the soil.

In fact, many intuitive people find that as the Moon grows brighter, their actual dreams become clearer and easier to understand, as the Universe is responding to the intentions we've been sending out. In the way that Spring begins to make itself known through the sudden appearance of buds and blossoms on the trees, our attention at the Crescent Moon is drawn to the subtle, yet distinct changes happening in our midst.

The crescent is a symbol of the Triple Goddess, envisioned by Wiccans as the shining cup of her hand, holding within her palm the potential of the Universe. The Goddess is coming into her Maiden role at this time, her youthful energy full of the promise of blessings to come.

This phase is the ideal time for taking action in the direction of our goals—actually beginning, on the physical plane, the projects we've intended for on the spiritual plane. The energy here is one of action and projecting our intentions outward into the Universe.

This can mean relatively small steps, such as establishing a routine of checking job listings, or contacting people you know can assist you with whatever it is you're seeking to manifest. Be willing to meet new people and/or vary your usual routine in order to allow new possibilities to come into your awareness. Watch for opportunities related to your goal to show up during this time, and be sure to take advantage of them, as doing so confirms to the Universe that you truly do want what you've been intending for.

This is how we root our manifestations—by taking the individual steps toward our goal as they present themselves. Just as the Spring unfolds little by little, yet steadily over each passing day, so do the circumstances that lead to your success.

Magic during the Crescent Moon continues to be related to attraction and increase, but the energy begins to pick up the pace and move things into a somewhat more defined focus.

Be willing to revisit the seed of intention you planted at the New Moon and evaluate how it may seem to be taking shape. Work spells to strengthen your resolve to see things through, and to draw even more assistance from the Universe in the days to come.

Spellwork regarding creativity, business, and financial matters in general is favored at this time, as this is a fortuitous time to begin new ventures and step out into the unknown. Truly, anything you wish to draw to you is a good area of focus now.

If you have a lot of inspired ideas and are unsure where to start, sit with each one and tune into your intuition. Which has the most active energy behind it when you think of it? Try starting there.

You can also ask the Maiden for guidance in selecting and focusing on your goal. Those who like to work when the Moon is up can cast spells from midmorning until the hour after sundown.

Goddesses: All Maiden goddesses, such as Aphrodite (Greek), Aine (Irish), Idunn (Norse)

WAXING HALF

Continuing its outward expansion, the Moon finishes out its first quarter and reaches the midpoint between New and Full.

This phase corresponds to the late Spring / early Summer season celebrated at Beltane. There is a somewhat more fiery aspect to the energy here as the pace of growth quickens and activities are ramping up. The Beltane holiday takes the loving, co-creative relationship between the God and Goddess as its theme, and this energy can be harnessed not just for love or romance, but for any goals that involve people coming together to create something new or enhance an existing creation.

Alternatively, if your goal does not include collaborating with others, you may find yourself in more consistent co-creation with the Universe itself, discovering your "groove" as you continue to allow new opportunities related to your goal to flow into your experience.

At this point on the Wheel of the Year, those who live in northern climates see the trees suddenly coming to life as their new leaves transform the landscape. Likewise, in the growth cycle, the Half Moon aligns with the sprouting of leaves, which serve as a plant's "power station" by converting sunlight to fuel. This is the indication that this new life, which began as a seed, truly means to stick around.

It's an ideal time to begin building your own infrastructure related to your magical goals, whether this means creating more detailed plans, following through on initial opportunities, or gathering support from those who can be of assistance. The main idea here is a heightened emphasis on growth, and nurturing your newly-sprouted intention. What can you do to harness the increasing push of energy coming from the Moon to fuel your progress?

If you're not experiencing any evidence of manifestation yet, there may be various factors at play. Are you staying in touch with your intuition, and paying attention to subtle nudges from the Universe? Are unexpected circumstances or changes occurring in your daily life?

Remember that sometimes, occurrences that seem inconvenient or annoying in the moment turn out to be steps on the path to realizing the goal, though we have no way of knowing it yet. Do your best to be at peace and trust the Universe to work out the "how" and the "when" of your manifestation. If you are attached to specific expectations, you may be blocking the ability of what you desire to come into your life.

Magical work at the waxing Half Moon is generally related to gaining or strengthening partnerships with others, whether they be friends, romantic interests, or business associates. Improving physical health and general well-being is also favored now.

You may also feel guided to "boost" any spellwork begun at the New Moon, perhaps by lighting a candle to add new energy to the existing working, creating a luck charm with your goal in mind, or simply by visualizing the manifestation with increasing clarity. It's not too late to set brand-new intentions, either, as there's still time between now and the Full Moon for the waxing energy to influence your magic.

This is still a time of powerful potential. Midday to midnight are the hours to work with if you're timing your spells with the Moon's presence in the sky.

Goddesses: Athena (Greek), Bast (Egyptian), Rhiannon (Welsh)

WAXING HALF TO FULL (GIBBOUS)

Shortly after reaching the Half, or 2nd-quarter mark, it becomes clear that the Moon is nearly Full. People tend to notice the Moon more during this phase, as it emerges just after sunset and rises later into the night sky.

Energies begin to intensify at this time, with heightened emotions and sharper instincts manifesting at the conscious level. Many people experience an increase in precognitive dreams and intuitive "hits" in the days leading up to the Full Moon, and some have more trouble sleeping than at any other time of the lunar month.

The waxing gibbous Moon corresponds to the weeks surrounding the Summer Solstice, when the trees and other vegetation are practically exploding with lushness and the newborn animals begin to gain independence.

Magical intentions set at the New Moon and tended throughout the waxing phase are about to come into fruition, provided we continue to believe in our success. The Goddess is now coming into her Mother aspect, her womb growing larger as the Moon grows with each passing hour.

This sense of manifestation being just on the verge of arrival is represented by the bud stage of the growth cycle, which the waxing gibbous phase corresponds to. The vision of a soon-to-unfold flower is a powerful metaphor for the delicious anticipation of new creations coming forth. It is also a good lesson in the importance of patience and trust in divine timing, as you cannot hurry the flower's process.

In terms of spellwork, no further direct action on our part is truly necessary at this point, as the flower will develop on its own, but we can use this stretch of days to make preparations for the upcoming Full Moon celebration, when we will welcome the unfolding of our intentions. Of course, if your daily life presents you with opportunities or clear steps to take related to your goal, by all means move forward with them!

Magically, this is considered to be an "all-purpose" phase, but the work should still be harnessing projective energy and focus on increase and drawing what you desire into your life. If you feel guided to, you may want to give a final boost of energy to any work begun at any point in the waxing phase.

Be sure to also take time to note any progress that has become apparent so far, no matter how subtle. Give yourself a pat on the back for any and all actions you've taken in pursuit of your goal, regardless of whether they seem to have had any effect yet. Continue to pay attention to your dreams and your intuitive hunches for messages you may be receiving from the Universe related to your desires.

As for new intentions, the waxing gibbous Moon has a "quickening" energy to it, so spells cast now will manifest swiftly, particularly if they are simple and well-focused. This energy is best harnessed after sundown, and before the first stirrings of dawn.

Goddesses: Nuit (Egyptian), Asteria (Greek), Luna (Roman)

FULL MOON

The Full Moon is the most powerful phase of the entire lunar cycle. Even people who don't believe in magic are able to recognize that something is energetically "different" at the Full Moon, as they experience strong emotions, erratic behavior in themselves or others, or strange sleep patterns.

Those who do understand magic are in an excellent position to take advantage of these lunar energies and bring their desires into physical reality at this time. Many Witches find that the day of the Full Moon is the most magically potent day of the month, and may save spellwork related to particularly important goals for this occasion. Divination can also be particularly successful at this time, as can efforts to improve psychic abilities.

The Full Moon represents absolute abundance and the full promise of the growth cycle. This is the flowering stage in the world of plant life—the flourish of beauty confirming that the fruit is on its way. The Mother aspect of the Triple Goddess is in her full power now, lending her nurturing and tending energies to our manifestations in progress.

This phase also corresponds with Lughnasa, the first of the three harvest festivals on the Wheel of the Year and the cross-quarter day between Summer and Autumn. Agriculturally speaking, this is the harvest with the most promise, as we are just beginning to reap the benefits of what we planted at the beginning of the cycle, yet we know that the bulk of the bounty is yet to come.

In keeping with this harvest theme, many Wiccans and other Witches make a point of expressing gratitude in their Full Moon celebrations. You may wish to write a list of all that has benefited you over the past month and thank the Universe (or the Goddess and/or the God, or whatever concept or identity you connect with in terms of a "higher power") for these blessings. Doing so before making any new magical requests is a great way to both honor the Full Moon theme of abundance and raise your vibrational frequency to an optimal state before sending out your new intention.

As for the intentions you began this lunar cycle with, use this phase to once again acknowledge the progress made thus far, to clarify what it is you want to see happen next, and to realign yourself with the energies of accomplishing your goal.

Often, the co-creative nature of manifestation means that you may experience a "false start" or two, which helps you refine your vision of what is ultimately the best outcome. For example, maybe you landed an interview for a job, only to discover that the company is not a good fit for you. You can use this experience to help you visualize, to an even more specific degree, the career circumstances that will suit you best.

Any and all magical purposes are favored at the Full Moon. If you can't decide on a specific goal, however, you can try letting magical timing be your guide. As mentioned in Part One, each Full Moon is traditionally linked with the season, the month, and/or the Zodiac sign in which it occurs. So you can choose according to seasonal correspondences—working for material abundance on a Full Moon in Autumn, for example, or banishing health problems on a Winter Full Moon.

Alternatively, you might work with the Zodiac sign that the Full Moon is occurring in, or with the current Sun sign. For example, spells related to communication or travel are good to work during Gemini, while Leo is a time to work for love, children, and vacations. (You can find more information about these systems in the Tables of Correspondence at the end of this guide.)

If you decide to adopt a regular practice of linking the Full Moon to the Zodiac, try to be consistent with your choice of alignments, for better overall momentum. In other words, if you work a Full Moon "Gemini" spell when the Sun is in Gemini, you should then use Cancer as your magical guide at the next Full Moon, rather than switching to the sign the Moon is in.

Of course, there are no hard-and-fast rules surrounding any of this—you should always work for what you feel are the most pressing goals, regardless of the seasonal or Zodiac correspondences.

As with the New Moon, many Witches try to work as closely as possible to the exact moment that the Moon becomes Full for maximum magical advantage. However, this moment often occurs at midday or early in the morning, which can be pretty inconvenient, especially for covens holding an Esbat!

Since working under moonlight is also an ideal condition for magic, it can be just as effective to cast your spells several hours later, once the sun has set and the Moon has risen, or else the night before it turns Full. In fact, some would argue that the window of time is even wider, given that the lunar energies surrounding the Full Moon begin to intensify up to three days beforehand and linger for at least two days afterward.

Although it's widely agreed that it's better to work before the Moon turns Full than afterward, this is really entirely up to your degree of focused intention and your circumstances. There may be situations when you just aren't able to time your work according to ideal conditions—don't let that prevent you from celebrating the Full Moon and casting your spell with enthusiasm!

Goddesses: All Mother goddesses, such as Arianrhod (Welsh), Danu (Irish), Isis (Egyptian), Selene (Greek)

FULL TO WANING HALF (GIBBOUS)

Within a few days after the Full Moon, the strong lunar energies have clearly begun to recede, ebbing like the ocean waves just after high tide. Now begins the waning half of the cycle, as the Moon starts to disappear gradually into shadow.

The Autumn Equinox marks this turning toward the dark time of year, and the days become noticeably shorter than just weeks ago. The Mother Goddess has reached the point of full maturity along her path and now progresses onward to greater and greater wisdom.

The harvest is in full swing now as Autumn's bounty is reaped from the fields. The fully ripened fruit is gathered and put to use. What can't be used is left to drop to the ground where it will feed the animals and the soil.

This is a time to harvest the fruit of our magical efforts, which includes affirming and giving thanks for any manifestations that have arrived or are on the horizon. Be sure to enjoy everything that has come into your life, and celebrate your efforts on both the physical and non-physical planes.

This is also the time to release the energy of outward action, and align with the energy of inward reflection. Let go of any specific spellwork that has yet to come into fruition. This doesn't mean you should give up on your goals—just release any attachments you have to outcomes from this particular spell.

It may be that there is a larger timeline for the manifestation to occur than you'd like, but this is where patience and trust in Universal timing comes in. In the meantime, you can take advantage of the waning energies of the lunar cycle to make some very beneficial changes in your life.

Eliminating negative energies and experiences is the governing principle of magic during the waning Moon. Spellwork aimed at overcoming obstacles, resolving conflicts, and removing causes of illness is favored at this time. Looking within and examining our inner landscape brings about clarity, and can help us identify where we might make more effective choices around recurring issues, both in our spellwork and in our daily lives.

Think of this work in terms of the harvest—we sort through what we've brought about and discard anything that doesn't serve us. What we let go of is released back to the Earth and ultimately transformed into new life.

Generally, this is a metaphorical suggestion for doing inner work on the level of the psyche, but it can also apply literally to cleaning and clearing. So if you've got a cluttered closet or any other area of your home that's been needing a good purge, this is an excellent time to get it done. Clear out the old and make room for the new—you may be surprised by how much your energy and mood improve after a good clutter-clearing session!

If you're still preoccupied by a goal that hasn't been realized during this time, shift your focus to one of banishing obstacles and releasing resistance—including any resistance to the fact that it hasn't yet manifested. Remember that you get what you focus on, so if you're having trouble envisioning your manifestation without feeling anxious or disappointed, work a spell for releasing those negative feelings and attachments, since they are not serving you.

As the Moon wanes, the obstacles, problems, and negative thought patterns you're experiencing will also recede. As with the Full Moon, working magic at night when the Moon is actually visible is ideal.

Goddesses: Demeter (Greek), Ceres (Roman), Freya (Norse)

WANING HALF

Just as the waxing Half Moon is a time of ramping up the projective, active energies of growth, the waning Half is accompanied by an increase in the receptive, passive energies of release. The Moon rises later and later with each passing night, with less and less illumination.

This is the harvest phase of the growth cycle—no more new growth will occur until the next Spring begins, so it's time to gather any last remaining fruits of this season's labor. This phase also corresponds with the third and final harvest festival, Samhain, which is when we make our preparations for the dark, cold Winter months.

This is not a somber time, however (although for those who deeply dislike the cold, it can seem like it!). Witches embrace both the light and the dark—as well as the heat and the cold—as equal parts of the whole of our experience on Earth. So while the focus of our magic may be on the less fun or joyful aspects of life—dealing with the unwanted, breaking unhealthy habits, etc.—we can appreciate the happiness that such work will ultimately bring into our lives.

As mentioned above, spellwork during the waning Moon is aimed at banishing and/or releasing negative influences and circumstances. Depending on how you view your life, you may have a fairly long list of things that fall into these categories! So how do you choose where to start?

For some, the process of deciding what to tackle at this time can feel overwhelming and even lead to despair. But there's no need to let the tricky work of addressing difficult issues get you down. For one thing, you're never expected to clear up all negativity from your life in one fell swoop! The work of removing what you don't want is similar to the work of attracting what you do want—your focus can't be on all things at the same time.

Happily, there will always be another two weeks of waning lunar energy to harness during the Moon's next cycle. With this in mind, you can make some wise decisions about your magical aims by taking one of the following approaches.

First, is there anything going on with you that needs immediate attention, such as a case of the flu, or a mechanical issue with your car? If so, the waning Half Moon is a perfect time to work a spell for releasing and resolving these problems.

If there are no immediately pressing issues, then simply identify a goal that feels achievable to you at this time. Perhaps it's releasing an addictive relationship with a particular food, or escaping unnecessary interactions with an annoying coworker. For bigger, more challenging problems, it's advisable to wait until the Crescent or even Dark Moon to set your intentions.

Many Witches find that the further the Moon wanes, the stronger its power to banish, remove, and release the unwanted. So use the first half of the waning phase for somewhat lighter work around release and removal, and use your successes to fuel your energy and confidence for the more powerful magic you want to work at the end of this lunar cycle.

Night is still the best time for casting your spells, and you can still catch the moon in the night sky for a few more evenings, before it begins to rise quite late.

Goddesses: the Cailleach (Celtic), Nepthys (Egyptian), Hella (Norse)

WANING CRESCENT

The waning Crescent Moon is the final point on the lunar cycle when the Moon is still visible at all, before it disappears completely into its Dark days.

This Crescent corresponds to the time of the Winter Solstice, or Yule—the festival of light that serves to remind us that new light, and new life, will come again at Winter's end. It also corresponds to the compost phase of the growth cycle—when the remaining, decaying plant matter is transformed into nutrients in the soil for the next generation of life to make use of.

Energetically, this is a very powerful time for conquering negative circumstances through release and removal. Magical work related to protection, banishing, and binding troublesome people or situations is favored now.

However, be careful not to adopt an attitude of conflict or battle when it comes to the issues you're working to resolve. If you see yourself as being engaged in an active fight, you will most likely reinforce the negative conditions, rather than releasing them.

For example, if your goal is to remove a major illness, keep your focus on how you will feel when you are well, rather than on "fighting" how you feel now. This is another instance where keeping the Law of Attraction in mind can really help you shape your magic. If you feel inclined, ask for assistance from the Crone Goddess, whose energies of wisdom and clear thinking are best suited for dealing with endings and removal.

It's also useful to keep the metaphor of composting in mind here. Although what we are releasing is not desirable or useful to us, it can be transformed into neutral or even beneficial energy in the larger world.

If you think about it, you don't resent the existence of a banana peel or a rotten tomato simply because you can't eat them! They may be unpleasant to the senses, but that doesn't mean they are inherently "bad." In fact, they can be turned to good if they are allowed to decompose and therefore nourish the soil.

Similarly, everything we release has had its own purpose—including conflicts, illness, and other challenges. What we learn from our struggles is just as useful as what we enjoy about our successes.

For example, let's say you're working to recover from a painful breakup of a romantic relationship. You might want to start with a spell to release your attachments to the past, and then move on to work related to healing the feelings that are hurting you right now.

However, don't put any energy into resentment about what happened, or fear of what's coming next. Work for acceptance of things as they are, and know that this experience will help you to navigate the next relationship along your path.

If you need to protect yourself from a person who is a harmful influence in your life, you can do a binding spell to keep them out of your way, but don't wish them harm in return.

For one thing, this isn't necessary for your spellwork to succeed—in fact, negative intent will most likely lead your spell to backfire.

When it comes to conflicts of any kind, a good general rule of thumb is to work for the best outcome for all involved, rather than trying to "win" or prove that you're right.

Waning magic is still ideal to work at night, but timing to align with the Moon's presence in the sky is tricky, since this Crescent won't rise until 3 a.m. That's a difficult time for most people to pull off any spellwork (but if you're able to, go for it)! If you're an early riser, you might try working just before dawn, instead, as the Moon will still be climbing in the sky at that point.

Goddesses: All Crone goddesses, such as Hecate (Greek), Cerridwen (Welsh), the Morrigan (Irish)

DARK MOON

During the final stretch of days before the Moon turns New again, it cannot be seen at all in the sky. This is often experienced as a quiet, yet fairly strange time, when energy levels fluctuate, logic becomes "fuzzy," and progress toward our goals can seem to be at a standstill.

In the Wheel of the Year alignments, this phase has no season or Sabbat, as we are dealing with the Moon's absence rather than its presence. However, it can be thought of as the period of time between the Winter Solstice and Imbolc, which in northern climates is often called the "dead" of Winter.

In the growth cycle alignments, the Dark Moon corresponds to the period of rest between growing cycles—a time to let the soil be, so that its nutrients can be replenished before it's time to plant new seeds.

This phase is also known as the "Balsamic Moon" in many traditions. The origins of the word "balsamic" are rooted in concepts related to healing, soothing, and restoring.

Many Witches use this period in exactly this way, refraining from actively working magic while they relax and refresh their energy for the next waxing phase. This can be a time for reading up on new magical techniques and approaches, as well as practicing divination and meditation.

In some traditions, the Dark Moon is the ideal time for past life regression, for the purpose of finding answers and insights regarding current challenges. Communicating with ancestors and loved ones in the spirit world can be especially productive during these days.

Abstaining from spellwork is certainly not mandatory, however. Plenty of people find the Dark Moon to be the best time for magic related to closure, or bringing things full circle.

We are still in the realm of the Crone, so this is a powerful time for releasing any karmic patterns that crop up again and again in your life, such as those related to lack, abandonment, betrayal, etc.

There is a destructive potential to the energy now that can be harnessed for these purposes. As always, remember to focus your intent on eliminating the situation itself, rather than aiming negativity at any people involved.

If you're timing your magic with the Moon's presence in the sky (invisible though it may be), work spells between three in the morning and three in the afternoon. And if you're having a difficult time for any reason during this phase, remember that the New Moon, and therefore a new beginning, is just around the corner.

Goddesses: All Crone goddesses

CHARTING YOUR OWN COURSE

Hopefully, you now have a clearer appreciation for the ever-shifting lunar energies associated with the cycles of the Moon and their magical implications.

Witches have long known that when we work with these rhythms of waxing and waning, we can align our magic with the projective and receptive currents of the tidal flow of the Universe. We learn to honor the roles of both creation and destruction in the cycles of Nature, and recognize that each has its part to play in the larger process of manifestation.

By choosing to follow the path of the Moon as an integral part of your magical practice, you are stepping into a rich tradition, begun long ago by our ancestors who implicitly understood the inherent power of Earth's celestial companion. Over time, as you gain experience with this approach to magical living, you will find your own understanding of these lunar energies setting roots within your psyche, and flourishing during every phase of the cycle.

It's important to note that this does take time—don't expect to be completely in tune with the Moon's energy every single day starting tomorrow. In fact, don't even expect yourself to follow the path outlined above for an entire lunar cycle on your first try.

You can certainly aim for that if you wish to, but be sure not to let yourself get discouraged if you lose track of which phase the Moon is in for a few days. Especially for less experienced Witches, it may take a few full cycles—or more—before you start becoming aware of the more subtle shifts in lunar energy.

Most people can feel the New Moon and Full Moon fairly easily when they tune in, but other points of the cycle tend to take awhile to detect on a sixth-sense level. If you're just starting out on this journey, and especially if you're new to magic, you may want to decide to focus on just the waxing phase at first.

Make a point of honoring the New Moon and spend some time identifying and visualizing your goals. Plan for some related spellwork to be done at the waxing Crescent or the waxing Half. Take note of any results—including hunches, signs, and potential developments—and stay open to more as the Moon continues to wax.

Celebrate the Full Moon and reflect on your experience of following the lunar path up to this point. Don't forget to congratulate yourself for having come this far! Then, decide how you'd like to approach the waning phase.

If it's starting to feel overwhelming, or like a chore rather than an enlightening experiment, take a break and plan to focus on the waning phase the next time it comes around. That's the beauty of cycles—they never end, so there will always be another opportunity for learning and growing in your practice.

WORKING FOR LARGER
GOALS OVER SEVERAL CYCLES

As acknowledged above, many—if not most—manifestations have a longer timeline than one lunar cycle could ever allow for.

You're very unlikely to be able to apply for *and* get into college, build your dream house, or write a best-selling novel from start to finish within the two week waxing cycle. Even goals that could theoretically be realized in this time frame, such as landing a good job, may take longer for a variety of reasons.

Perhaps the job of your dreams is on its way, but the person currently in the position has yet to give their resignation notice. Or it could be that your ideal romantic match won't be moving to your city for another few months.

So don't conclude that your spellwork failed simply because the Full Moon has come and gone and you can't yet see the evidence of your success!

(Furthermore, don't assume that the days around the Full Moon are the only window of opportunity for manifestations to reveal themselves. Although the waning phase is traditionally a time to focus on releasing things from our lives, plenty of fortunate circumstances can, and do, come into our experience during this time as well.)

So what should you do with those larger intentions as the next New Moon comes around? Should you keep working spells for love, prosperity, career advancement, etc., during every lunar cycle until your goals are realized?

The answer really depends on how you go about it. If you're repeating the same spell over and over, then you're likely telling the Universe (and yourself) that you don't believe your prior efforts have set anything in motion, even though events and circumstances may very well be shaping up to bring you what you desire. This can set you up for an endless cycle of starting over, so that you're blocking any progress that would otherwise be making its way to you.

A wiser approach would be to experiment with different kinds of spellwork from Moon to Moon, still focusing on your goal but from the perspective of adding new and various layers of energy to the initial spell. For example, you might work a candle spell for financial abundance during the first cycle, and then create a charm for the same outcome during the next waxing Moon, which you can carry with you for the duration of two more lunar cycles.

Be sure to take note of any manifestations, no matter how small or seemingly insignificant, throughout the process. This can be a great way to develop your magical talent, explore new methods, and discover what kinds of spellwork suit you best.

Finally, keep in mind that larger, multi-cycle manifestations happen in steps.

If your goal is a new career, for example, you might first be prompted to enroll in some classes related to your desired field. Let that be your focus for one lunar cycle, working spells to boost your success in your new studies.

Next, you might focus on finding help polishing up your resume. Focusing on the individual steps not only helps you take action in the material world, but also helps you specify the focus of your magic as you patiently allow the larger goal—the brand-new, exciting and fulfilling job—to unfold according to right timing.

The same is true for waning Moon goals. If you're like most people, you probably aren't going to completely get over the end of a significant relationship all in one waning cycle. But you can work to release your emotional attachments and heal your grief one step at a time, allowing the rhythms of the lunar cycle to guide your journey.

Indeed, the Moon's never-ending cycles can provide a comforting and nurturing structure for us as we witness the unfolding of all of our manifestations, no matter how long they take to come to fruition.

GETTING CREATIVE WITH TIMING

There's one potential "glitch" in the system of working with lunar alignments that every Witch will encounter at one point or another—the inconvenience of unexpected obstacles.

In other words, what happens when your immediate needs are at odds with the current Moon phase?

What if you need to work a spell for fast cash for a car repair, or some other expense that simply won't wait until the Moon is waxing again? Or, what if there's a conflict that needs resolution, but it's only a few days after the waxing Crescent?

Does this mean there is no magical recourse available to you in these instances? Of course not!

First of all, the Moon phase alignments are guidelines, rather than absolute rules. They add tremendous power to your spellwork, but the Universe is infinitely vast and infinitely capable of responding to your magical requests no matter where the Moon is in relation to the Earth.

So don't ever feel that your spell won't work at all because it's the wrong phase of the lunar cycle. As long as your energy is sufficiently focused on your intention—and if your need is great enough to warrant working against the lunar tides—then you will succeed.

However, it will help enormously if you can design your spellwork to be as compatible as possible with the current Moon phase, no matter the specific goal. Again, it's really all about how you approach your intention.

For example, let's say you're just chomping at the bit to work a prosperity spell, but the Moon is on the wane. Odds are that your strong desire to focus on this area of your life is coming from a sense of lack, or a belief that you never have enough money.

This is a great time for spellwork to release this "scarcity thinking," which, due to the Law of Attraction, is essentially the driving force behind all money woes.

In the case of the needed car repair, you can view the situation as an obstacle to be banished, rather than as a specific need for money. Remember, you never know *how* a manifestation might occur, so focusing on the outcome, rather than on the financial need, makes much magical sense during the waning Moon.

Feeling a need to release a relationship while the Moon is waxing? You can start with spellwork focused on building your inner strength and increasing your self-care, so that you'll have the courage and resolve it takes to make a clean break of it.

It's still recommended to wait for the waning Moon to do the actual breaking off, or releasing, but if you've been preparing during the waxing Moon by attracting the right frame of mind, you will be better able to bide your time until the lunar energies are in alignment with your goal.

As you can no doubt see by now, shaping your magic to harmonize with the Moon's movements around the Earth is an art that takes patience and practice. Working with the lunar energies of each phase of the cycle, and tailoring your spellwork to best align with either the waxing or waning currents, is not a skill you can learn overnight.

However, if you put in the time and the effort, you will certainly begin to see results in short order. It won't be long until you're moving naturally with the rhythms of the Moon, learning to relate intuitively to each phase of the cycle in equal turn.

Once you've gotten these basics down, then you'll be ready to have even more fun with the rare lunar events that come around just a few times a year (or less!), which we'll take a brief look at next.

BLUE MOONS AND LUNAR ECLIPSES

Although every Full Moon is a time of heightened magical power, there are two types of events that bring extra special energy to these lunar occasions: Blue Moons and Lunar Eclipses.

These rare occurrences often drum up plenty of attention within the mainstream world, but Witches are the ones who know how to harness their energy for magical success.

These two events differ in key ways. For instance, Blue Moons occur as a result of how we measure the solar year, while Lunar Eclipses are a function of the Earth's and Moon's orbits in space.

A Blue Moon is not actually blue and doesn't look any different from any other Full Moon, whereas a Lunar Eclipse can be quite noticeable, provided it occurs during nighttime hours.

Regardless of these differences, however, both of these lunar events are important to many Wiccans and other Witches, who make a point of observing them through ritual and spellwork on those rare occasions when they appear.

BLUE MOONS

You've no doubt heard the phrase "once in a Blue Moon" used to describe something that only happens very infrequently.

The origins of the term "Blue Moon" are thought to come from a few different possible sources, beginning with references going back to the 16th century and ultimately ending up in the titles of novels, songs, and even a flavor of ice cream.

Interestingly, the phrase initially referred to something that was completely impossible, used in the same way that people today might use "when pigs fly." However, there have in fact been documented cases of the Moon appearing blue in the sky, as a result of dust or smoke particles in the atmosphere from volcanoes and forest fires.

Of course, our modern concept of Blue Moons has nothing to do with the Moon's visual appearance, but rather with the Moon turning Full at an irregular time as measured by the yearly calendar—an "extra" Full Moon of sorts.

There are two different systems for identifying a Blue Moon. The first comes from farmer's almanacs of the 19th and early 20th centuries, which listed the Full Moons of each year using names borrowed from Native American traditions (many of which are now incorporated into Wiccan and other Pagan practices, as we saw in Part One).

Typically, there are three Full Moons in each season, or quarter, of the year—from the Winter Solstice to the Spring Equinox, for example.

When four Full Moons occurred in this period, the almanacs would call the third of the four a Blue Moon. These seasonal Blue Moons occur roughly every 2 to 3 years.

The second and more well-known type of Blue Moon is the second Full Moon of a calendar month. These occur with roughly every 32 to 33 months, and every 19 years or so we see two Blue Moons within one calendar year.

Most contemporary Witchcraft traditions around the Blue Moon observe the two-in-one-month version. But whether you consider the monthly or the seasonal Blue Moon to be the real deal (and why not go with both?), there's plenty of magical opportunity on these special occasions.

Many Wiccans view the Blue Moon as a time of heightened connection with the Goddess. Spells worked at this time are considered to have far more potency than typical Full Moon spells. Some Witches even believe that the effects of spellwork done at this time can have effects lasting until the next Blue Moon!

In particular, magic related to wisdom, love, and protection is effective on a Blue Moon, as are all forms of divination. And if you have any dreams that you have previously considered impossible to achieve, this is the perfect time to give spellwork a try!

LUNAR ECLIPSES

Less rare, but perhaps far more powerful than a Blue Moon is a Full Moon Lunar Eclipse, which happens generally twice a year (though some years may see three or more, depending on the circumstances).

Lunar Eclipses occur when the Earth's shadow blocks the light from the Sun, which would otherwise be illuminating the Moon.

There are three types of Eclipses—partial, penumbral, and total.

A partial Lunar Eclipse occurs when only part of the Moon enters the inner section of the Earth's shadow, called the umbra. The outer section of the shadow is the penumbra, and when the Moon passes only through this section it's called a penumbral Eclipse.

Total Lunar Eclipses occur when the Moon moves completely into the innermost, darkest part of the umbra, and these are the most visually stunning. Aside from seeming to almost disappear, the Moon can take on a vivid reddish hue during total Eclipses, depending on the atmospheric conditions.

In terms of magical energy, any of the three types are excellent occasions for extra special spellwork, but the total Lunar Eclipse is considered by many to be the most powerful lunar event of all.

Why is this? During a total Eclipse, the Moon appears to move through its entire lunar cycle in the span of just a few hours. As it moves through the Earth's shadow, it appears to wane, disappear, then reappear and wax again until Full.

This means that you can tap into each phase of the Moon's cycle in a brief period of time, rather than over the course of a month. You can do work for increase and decrease in one sitting if you like, or set new intentions for one aspect of your life while celebrating the culmination of another.

And if you're lucky enough to be able to actually watch the Eclipse in the night sky, well, that's about as magical as it gets! But don't be discouraged if you're not personally able to view it—the energetic benefits of the Eclipse are still available to you, if you wish to harness it through magical work.

Likewise, if you can perform your spells during the time of the actual Eclipse, whether or not it's visible in the sky, this is ideal, but if not, try to work after sundown, once the Full Moon has risen.

So what kind of magic is best to work during a Lunar Eclipse? As with any Full Moon, this is an all-purpose lunar phase, so anything you wish to work for is perfectly appropriate. However, many Witches find that a few specific areas are especially suited to Eclipse energy and spellwork related to these areas is particularly powerful.

Anything around healing, on all levels—physical, emotional, and spiritual—is good to intend for now, as is any work related to personal growth and/or spiritual development.

If you've been seeking to establish a relationship with a particular aspect of the God or Goddess, this is a good time to make offerings and spend time in meditation. Be open to subtle (and sometimes not-so-subtle) shifts in your energy as the deity responds to your request for contact. If the deity was primarily associated with the Moon in their original culture—such as Selene (Greek) or Toth (Egyptian)—this is highly likely to result in a powerful experience.

Finally, any magical activity that specifically honors or makes use of the Moon's energy, such as creating talismans and charging them in moonlight or taking a Full Moon ritual bath, has tremendous energetic effect during a Lunar Eclipse.

ENDLESS POSSIBILITIES

As we have now seen, the magic potential of the Moon is not limited to specific nights or special occasions.

It's true that most of us feel its gravitational pull more during the New and Full Moons than at other times, and there are extremely powerful Blue Moons and Lunar Eclipses that amplify the lunar energy a few times per year.

But in actuality, every single day of the lunar cycle provides opportunities to align with the powerful energy of this celestial being. There is never a time when the Moon has no power—not even those days and nights when it seems to have disappeared completely.

Indeed, if you choose to, you can allow the Moon's energy to help you shape your approach to spellwork each and every day for the rest of your magical life!

So far, we have treated the practical aspects of lunar magic rather generally, in terms of choosing goals and tending your manifestations in harmony with the phases of the Moon. In Part Three, you'll find more specific, hands-on information to help you get on your way.

A few spells are included here, of course, as well as recipes for Moon-oriented magical oil blends; Tables of Correspondence for Moon-associated crystals, herbs, and flowers; methods for enhancing your personal connection with the Moon, and more.

As always, keep yourself attuned to your intuition's responses to what you read. If a particular spell, method, or ingredient piques your interest, then you've found your best avenue to your next magical lunar adventure!

PART THREE

A LUNAR GRIMOIRE

A MISCELLANY
OF MOON MAGIC

Since at least the days of ancient Mesopotamia, magical information has been kept in texts that eventually came to be known as "grimoires." A grimoire is a book where you can find spells, rituals, incantations, recipes for potions, mystical symbols, keys to divination systems and just about anything else that fits under the "occult" umbrella.

The Wiccan version of the grimoire is, of course, the Book of Shadows, which is part of both coven and solitary traditions throughout the Wiccan world. You may already have one of your own, or you may be just beginning to compile information that will ultimately be included in your personal grimoire.

You can think of this final section of this guide as a short version of a "lunar" Book of Shadows. Each of the first four spells is focused on one of the four quarters of the lunar cycle, followed by spells for a Blue Moon and a Lunar Eclipse.

You'll also find a quick Table of Correspondence for spell ingredients associated with the Moon, for help in designing your own lunar spells. Suggested magical purposes to focus on during specific Moon phases and Zodiac locations can help you choose the most promising goals to work for at any given point in time.

Of course, there are other ways of working with the Moon beyond casting spells. To that end, pointers on lunar gardening, charging tools in moonlight, and creating your own Moon-associated magical oils and bath salts are included here. You'll also find a few suggestions for creating your own rituals of communing with the Moon, to help you deepen your spiritual connection to its energies.

Keep in mind, this is just a brief sample of the possibilities when it comes to lunar magic, but there's plenty here to get you started and inspire you to build your own practice.

A DAILY RITUAL
FOR GREETING THE MOON

The best way to develop your own personal relationship with the Moon is to interact with it directly, every day. Try integrating this brief ritual into your daily life for the entirety of one lunar cycle.

This is especially useful for those who are just starting to get acquainted with Moon magic, Wicca, or any other Nature-based spiritual path. It can take as little as two minutes, or longer if you like, depending on when you're able to work it into your schedule from day to day.

You will need to know when to expect the Moon to be visible in your area in order to plan. This information can easily be found online, and you can also refer to the rising and setting times chart at the end of Part Three for a rough guide.

For best results, stand outside under the Moon and gaze directly at it. If this isn't possible, look at it through a window.

Truly look at it. See if you notice any new details about its exact shape, its shadowy features, and its changing image as it disappears behind passing clouds, then reemerges.

Even if it's raining, you can still get a general sense of where the Moon is in the sky, so aim your focus there. If the Moon simply isn't in the sky at any point when you're awake, close your eyes and visualize it—as it appears in its current phase—as clearly as you can.

Spend some time silently communing with the lunar energy and when you feel ready, say the following words (or compose your own). If you're unable to do the ritual in private, you can say them silently.

"Today/tonight I greet you, Moon, with joy.
Thank you for your divine light,
your Goddess energy,
your sacred power.
I open myself to your mysteries
and welcome your eternal wisdom.
So let it be."

FOUR QUARTERS
MOON SPELL SERIES

This relatively simple spell is repeated throughout the lunar cycle, with variations appropriate to each phase.

While each of the four spells can certainly stand alone, there is a powerful advantage to working all of them for an entire lunar cycle, to establish an energetic pattern that aligns you with the Moon's rhythms.

You can tailor each working to your own practice by choosing your own combination of ingredients—feel free to substitute any of the suggested items below with other Moon-associated crystals, herbs, and flowers—and by stating your goals in your own words.

Each working might be focused on one aspect of the same overall goal, or the intentions for each spell may be unrelated to each other—it's all up to you.

You will need:

- 3 small pieces of moonstone, smoky quartz, and/or quartz crystal
- 1 teaspoon dried hibiscus, anise seed, lilac, and/or Irish moss
- 1 white tea light or spell candle
- 1 work candle (optional)

Instructions:

Light the work candle, if using.

Arrange the crystals in a triangle shape around the spell candle, and then use the herbs and/or flowers to create a circle encompassing the triangle.

Spend a few moments visualizing the Moon as it looks in its current phase. (You might want to place images of the Moon on your altar or work space for help.)

Now, visualize the outcome of manifesting your goal. When you feel ready, state your goal out loud, as if it has already come to be.

Light the spell candle, and seal the spell by saying the appropriate words below (or words of your own choosing):

1st quarter (New Moon):

> *"For my intention I plant these seeds,*
> *Knowing the Goddess will meet my needs."*

2nd quarter (Waxing Half):

> *"Day by day and night by night,*
> *My plans are growing with the light."*

3rd quarter (Full Moon):

> *"Abundant thanks for abundance blessed,*
> *and I know still more will manifest."*

4th quarter (Waning Half):

> *"I now release this _____ unwanted*
> *My mind is clear and my heart undaunted."*

Leave the candle to burn out on its own. Spell candles burn between 1-3 hours, while tea lights tend to last longer.

BLUE MOON
GOOD LUCK CHARM

Since the Blue Moon is indeed a rare occasion, you may as well make the most of it when it rolls around! Create a good luck charm infused with the lunar power of the Blue Moon, and keep it with you until the next one.

This spell draws on the energies of the color blue, which is infused with the qualities of peace, wisdom and protection, and often used in spellwork related to prosperity, health, and good luck.

You may want to add even more of this energy to the spell by decorating your altar or work space with blue fabrics, flowers, imagery, etc. and/or wearing blue yourself.

You will need:

- 1 blue votive or spell candle
- 7 small blue crystals, such as sodalite, lapis lazuli, aquamarine, blue calcite, turquoise, kyanite, and aqua aura
- Small piece of blue paper and pen (blue ink)
- Jasmine or sandalwood essential oil
- 1 small drawstring bag
- 1 work candle (white, silver, indigo or violet)

Instructions:

Place all of the ingredients on your altar or work space and light the work candle as you say:

"With great joy and faith I greet this Blue Moon."

Anoint the spell candle with the oil, and place it in its holder.

Write the following (or similar) words on the paper: *All good luck is mine.*

Fold the paper in half, and then half again.

Now, say the following (or similar) words and light the spell candle:

> *"On this rare night shines a rare light,*
> *the magical power of the Blue Moon.*
> *I draw this energy into my life*
> *and all that comes to me will be a boon."*

Place one drop of the oil on the paper, then put it in the drawstring bag.

Now pass each crystal, one by one, over the flame of the spell candle (high enough not to burn your fingers!) and place it gently in the bag.

Pull the bag closed and leave it in front of the spell candle until the candle has burned all the way down.

Keep your good luck charm with you on your person, in your car, or in a special place in your home.

At the next Blue Moon, unpack it, bury or burn the paper, and give thanks for all of your good luck!

LUNAR PAPER ECLIPSE SPELL

A Lunar Eclipse is a great time to work both waning and waxing magic in a single spell. In fact, it's very powerful to use both of these approaches on the same magical goal when harnessing Eclipse energy.

For example, if your focus is a health-related goal, you can release illness and attract strength and positive energy. If the intention is prosperity, you can release old limiting patterns or beliefs around money and attract new opportunities or surprise windfalls.

Use construction paper or scrap paper to make your circles. They don't have to be perfect circles, but the paper should be free of any text or images on both sides.

If you're working during a total Lunar Eclipse and want to acknowledge the blood-red color of the Moon at this time, use a dark red candle.

You will need:

- 1 black or dark red candle
- 1 small (3-4 inch) white paper circle
- 1 equally-sized black paper circle
- White and black crayons
- Fire-proof dish

Instructions:

Light the candle.

Write what you want to release on the black circle, using the white crayon.

Write what you intend to attract on the white circle with the black crayon.

Turn the circles over so the blank sides are facing you.

Now, pass the black circle over the white one, in the manner of a total Lunar Eclipse.

Pause briefly when the two circles are exactly aligned and say "*It is done.*"

Then continue the motion until the "paper Eclipse" is complete.

Carefully light the black circle with the candle flame and allow it to burn out in the dish (or in a sink).

You can bury the white circle, make it part of a new magical charm, or add it to a vision board to remind you of what you're bringing into your life with this powerful energy.

MAGICAL OIL BLENDS
FOR LUNAR OCCASIONS

Anoint magical tools and/or wear a few drops of these blends during your spellwork on the New and Full Moons. Using pure essential oils, rather than synthetics, is strongly recommended.

To prevent irritating your skin, be sure to use a carrier oil, such as almond, jojoba, or grapeseed oil, to dilute the essential oils.

Use 2 tablespoons of carrier oil per recipe.

Full Moon Oil Recipe:

- 4 drops jasmine
- 3 drops sandalwood
- 2 drops clary sage

New Moon Oil Recipe:

- 3 drops lemon
- 2 drops rose
- 2 drops sandalwood

*Blended oils will stay good for several months to one year, provided they're stored in a cool, dark place.

FULL MOON RITUAL
BATH SALTS

This bath ritual is perfect for a powerful night of Full Moon magic!

You will need:

- 3 tablespoons sea salt
- 1/4 teaspoons dried hibiscus petals
- 1/4 teaspoons dried mugwort leaves
- 1/8 teaspoons anise seed
- 2-3 drops lavender oil

Instructions:

Place the salt in a small bowl.

Place the herbs in a mortar and pestle and gently crush while combining thoroughly.

Pour them into the bowl with the salt and stir again.

Add the oil and stir again.

Add to the bath under running water.

*Note: if your drain clogs easily, use a mesh strainer to catch the herbs when you're finished with your bath.

CHARGING TOOLS WITH LUNAR ENERGY

Of the many methods for infusing your ritual tools and spell ingredients with magical energy, charging them under the light of the Moon is one of the simplest and most effective.

Moonlight is known to have both cleansing and charging properties, so you don't have to worry about clearing the old energy from your items as a separate step.

For best results, leave your tools out overnight under the Full Moon, or at least in a windowsill where they will receive direct moonlight.

Lunar energy is particularly suited to charging crystals and other mineral stones—particularly those associated with intuitive and psychic abilities. You can really see and feel the effect of the Moon on your crystals the next day—they'll be shiny and new and feel great in your hand!

GARDENING WITH THE MOON

One of the most rewarding ways to tap into the rhythms of lunar energies is through growing your own herbs, vegetables, and flowers.

Whether you've got a sprawling outdoor garden or a few pots on a windowsill, you can work with the phases of the Moon's cycle for optimal success.

Gardening and farming according to lunar phases is rooted in age-old folklore, as our ancestors observed the Moon's effects on their crops.

Of course, we now know that the Moon's gravitational pull on the oceans is also felt in the Earth's subtle bodies of water, which in turn affect the soil. But even if your soil is contained within a garden bed or a pot, the energetic connection you're making to the Moon brings a "green thumb" effect to your efforts!

If you're able, try growing some moon-associated plants, or other magical herbs, to have on hand for an extra boost to your spellwork.

First Quarter (New to waxing Half): This is the best time to plant above-ground crops that produce seeds outside of the fruit, such as grain crops, broccoli and other cruciferous vegetables, spinach and other greens, and most annual herbs.

Second Quarter (waxing Half to Full): Plant above-ground crops that produce their seeds inside the fruit or seed pod, such as beans, tomatoes, peppers, and squash. The two to three days before the Full Moon are the "sweet spot" for planting during this period.

106

Third Quarter (Full to waning Half): As the waning phase begins, particularly in the first few days after the Full Moon, the time is perfect for planting root vegetables like carrots, potatoes, beets and onions. Bulbs, perennials, and biennials are favored now as well.

Fourth Quarter (waning Half to Dark): This phase is best for weeding, harvesting, pruning, and transplanting crops. Give your houseplants a little extra love at this time as well, and then let everything rest—yourself included!—for a few days before the New Moon.

*Note: if you're working strictly with potted herbs and flowers, or if all of your outdoor plants are of the same type, you can still tend them according to the basic patterns of waxing and waning. Plant, fertilize, and gently weed during the waxing phase, and prune, harvest, and transplant during the waning.

TABLES OF CORRESPONDENCE

Included here are brief tables of correspondence, relevant to anyone looking to work with the Moon's magical energies.

ZODIAC SIGNS
AND MAGICAL PURPOSES

These are the most common magical purposes associated with the Moon as it relates to each sign of the Zodiac.

Of course, to make use of these correspondences you'll need to know which sign the Moon is in at any given time! You can find this information online, or in a Wiccan or other Pagan resource, such as the annual *Witch's Almanac* (see "Suggestions for Further Reading" at the end of this guide).

A good source will also identify when the Moon is void of course, or between signs. Some Witches find that working during void of course periods leads to less effective magic, while others experience no difficulty with spells cast at these times. You may want to experiment with this, and see what works best for you.

Moon in Zodiac Sign	Work Magic Related to...
Aries	new ventures, general health and vitality, self-improvement, difficult conflicts, navigating issues with bureaucracy, leadership, authority, impatience difficult tempers, surgery
Taurus	money, prosperity, real estate, material acquisitions, self-esteem, love, sensuality, gardening and farming, fertility, patience, endurance, commitment, music, the arts, business

Moon in Zodiac Sign	Work Magic Related to...
Gemini	intelligence, communication, commerce, siblings, writing, teaching, neighbors, dealing with gossip, travel, transportation, public relations, media, networking, adaptability, memory, LGBT issues
Cancer	home, family, mothers, children, traditions, weather and climate, security, integrity, water issues (particularly natural bodies of water), psychic abilities, integrity, listening to and assisting others
Leo	love (platonic), self-confidence, self-expression, performing in public, vacation and leisure time, courage, childbirth, taking risks, good cheer, gambling, amusement, creativity, loyalty, fine arts
Virgo	health and healing, diet, business and trade, tools, employment, intelligence and intellect, co-workers, military and police, exercise and fitness, work ethic, debt, cleansing and purification, hunting, pets
Libra	legal matters, justice, marriage, peace, balance, diplomacy, beauty, harmony, team-building, contracts, romance and dating, partnership, art and music, socializing, meeting people, overcoming laziness
Scorpio	regeneration, renewal, sex, death, secrets, divination, psychic development, banishing, willpower, purification, hypnotism, emotional honesty, solitude, courage, transformation, mediumship

Moon in Zodiac Sign	Work Magic Related to...
Sagittarius	optimism, resilience, generosity, legal matters, education (especially higher education), ethics, dreams, contacting the divine, generosity, fame, publishing, good luck, long journeys, fun, humor, languages
Capricorn	careers, jobs, promotions, fathers, responsibility, solitude, healing from depression, ambition, public recognition, honor, reputation, awards, long term results, government, time management, wisdom
Aquarius	friendship, acquaintances, politics, electronics, freedom, science, extrasensory development, breaking bad habits, problem solving, objectivity, luck, meeting new people, social justice, hope
Pisces	psychic ability, music, spirituality, criminal matters, widows and orphans, reversing bad luck, finding lost items, charity, self-reflection, past lives, facing fears, endings, water (particularly oceans and salt water), dance, drug and alcohol problems

SEASONAL ASSOCIATIONS AND MAGICAL PURPOSES

These correspondences can be applied in a few different ways. As discussed in Part Two, each phase of the lunar cycle corresponds to one of the four seasons. So if the Moon is waxing, for example, you can choose a magical purpose for Spring.

Of course, you can also break it down into the eight "seasons," or Sabbats, for more flexibility, and a more evenly aligned distribution around the Wheel of the Year.

If the Moon is at waxing Half, feel free to look to the Summer correspondences in addition to those for Spring.

Finally, you might simply work according to the actual season you're in! This approach is especially effective at the Full Moon.

Moon Phase—Seasonal Association	Work Magic Related to...
Spring	healing, fertility, purification, gardening, environmental concerns, psychic ability, paying debts and bills
Summer	friendship, love, marriage, strength, physical stamina, protection, courage, beauty
Autumn	employment, money, real estate, material acquisitions, transformation, reaping benefits from past efforts
Winter	breaking bad habits, banishment, releasing emotional difficulties, magical study and introspection

SPELL INGREDIENTS ASSOCIATED WITH THE MOON

These are the most common colors, crystals, flowers, herbs, incense, and oils associated with the Moon. There are more of each, of course, which you can find in your own further explorations!

Colors	Crystals	Flowers
Silver	Moonstone	Hyacinth
White	Pearl	Hibiscus
Royal Blue	Smoky Quartz	Lily
Indigo	Selenite	Lilac
Violet	Quartz Crystal	Iris
Grey	Meteorite	Lotus

Herbs	Incense	Oils
Moonwort	Sandalwood	Lemon Balm
Mugwort	Myrrh	Jasmine
Fennel	Lavender	Sandalwood
Anise Seed	White Sage	Camphor
Evening Primrose	Vervain	Rose
Irish Moss	Jasmine	Clary Sage

RISING AND SETTING TIMES FOR THE MOON

This is a very basic tracking tool for learning to find the Moon in the sky on a daily basis. You can find exact rising and setting times for where you live online. Eventually, as you get into a practice of locating the Moon throughout the course of its cycle, you'll develop an instinctual feel for when to expect—and not to expect—the Moon to appear in your view of the sky.

Moon Phase	Moon Rise	Moon Set
New	Sunrise	Sunset
1st Quarter	Local Noon	Local Midnight
Full	Sunset	Sunrise
3rd Quarter	Local Midnight	Local Noon

CONCLUSION

Hopefully, you are coming away from this guide with a much broader perspective on the Moon than you had before.

Its magical energies, its influence over all life on Earth, and its potential to aid you in manifesting your dreams make this celestial body well worth paying attention to! Of course, as we have seen, you are influenced by the moon whether you pay it any mind or not.

In fact, many Witches and "ordinary folk" alike have remarked that when they keep at least one eye on where the Moon is in its cycle, their lives are less full of roadblocks and unpleasant surprises.

When they forget about the Moon for awhile, life can start to get more chaotic. What many don't realize is that by noticing and acknowledging the Moon, they are attuning to its energies, and therefore living more in harmony with the rhythms of Nature.

Each day provides you with an opportunity to take a moment to connect with the Moon, whether through a formal ritual or a brief, silent greeting. Each phase of the Moon's cycle offers particular energies that you can attune with and harness for your specific magical goals.

This lunar approach to magic offers a richly diverse, yet comfortably cyclical path for you to follow as you continue your never-ending explorations of ritual and spellwork. But whether or not you decide to adopt a structured practice of lunar magic, you will certainly benefit from keeping these rhythms in your consciousness on a regular basis.

If you would like to learn more about Moon magic, be sure to check out some of the sources listed on the following. May the light of the Goddess and the magic of the Moon be with you on your journey!

SUGGESTIONS FOR FURTHER READING

The topic of Moon magic has been written about widely, by Wiccan authors and others who work with the Moon as part of their magical practice.

While you'll no doubt find similar, basic information about the energies and correspondences of the lunar phases in many of these resources, each author has their own individual experiences and perspective on these topics.

As with anything else in Wicca or the larger Pagan world, it's always worth the effort to learn as much as you can in order to deepen your own practice.

This brief list of books offers some solid places to start, as well as a few suggested resources for helping you keep close track of the Moon in your day-to-day life. Happy reading!

Books:

These general sources cover some of the topics from this guide in more detail, as well as plenty of additional Moon lore, from a range of perspectives. For those interested in learning more about the role of astrology in working with the Moon's energies, the last two books are well worth checking out.

Diane Ahlquist, *Moon Spells: How to Use the Phases of the Moon to Get What You Want* (2002)

Zsuzsanna E. Budapest, *Grandmother Moon: Lunar Magic in Our Lives—Spells, Rituals, Goddesses, Legends, and Emotions Under the Moon* (1991)

D.J. Conway, *Moon Magick: Myth & Magic, Crafts & Recipes, Rituals & Spells* (1995)

Dorothy Morrison, *Everyday Moon Magic: Spells & Rituals for Abundant Living* (2003)

Rachel Patterson, *Pagan Portals - Moon Magic* (2014)

Yasmin Boland, *Moonology: Working with the Magic of Lunar Cycles* (2016)

Ann Moura, *Mansions of the Moon for the Green Witch: A Complete Book of Lunar Magic* (2010)

Almanacs and Calendars

In addition to detailed daily information about the Moon's current phase and Zodiac sign, each of these annual publications contains articles on a diverse range of topics of interest to Wiccans and other Witches.

The almanacs in particular are actually worth hanging onto as references long after their calendar information becomes outdated. In fact, you can still find the 2012 Witches' Almanac, which is focused on all things Moon-related, at online retailers.

The datebooks and calendars provide the lunar phase information in a readily-accessible format for easier integration of the cycle into your daily life. These are not the only resources that include these details, however, so feel free to shop around for other possibilities as well!

Llewellyn's Magical Almanac: Practical Magic for Everyday Living (Annual Publication)

The Witches' Almanac (Annual Publication)

The Witches' Almanac: Issue 32—Wisdom of the Moon (Witches' Almanac: Complete Guide to Lunar Harmony) (2012)

Llewellyn's Witches' Datebook (Annual Planner)

Llewellyn's Witches' Calendar (Wall Calendar)

FREE AUDIOBOOK PROMOTION

Don't forget, you can now enjoy a free audiobook version of any of my books when you start a free 30-day trial with Audible. This includes best-sellers such as *Wicca for Beginners* and *Wicca Book of Spells*.

Members receive free audiobooks every month, as well as exclusive discounts. And, if you don't want to continue with Audible, just remember to cancel your membership. You won't be charged a cent, and you'll get to keep your book!

To download this or any of my 20+ books on Wicca and related topics, simply visit:

www.wiccaliving.com/free-audiobook

Happy listening!

MORE BOOKS BY LISA CHAMBERLAIN

Wicca for Beginners: A Guide to Wiccan Beliefs, Rituals, Magic, and Witchcraft

Wicca Book of Spells: A Book of Shadows for Wiccans, Witches, and Other Practitioners of Magic

Wicca Herbal Magic: A Beginner's Guide to Practicing Wiccan Herbal Magic, with Simple Herb Spells

Wicca Book of Herbal Spells: A Book of Shadows for Wiccans, Witches, and Other Practitioners of Herbal Magic

Wicca Candle Magic: A Beginner's Guide to Practicing Wiccan Candle Magic, with Simple Candle Spells

Wicca Book of Candle Spells: A Book of Shadows for Wiccans, Witches, and Other Practitioners of Candle Magic

Wicca Crystal Magic: A Beginner's Guide to Practicing Wiccan Crystal Magic, with Simple Crystal Spells

Wicca Book of Crystal Spells: A Book of Shadows for Wiccans, Witches, and Other Practitioners of Crystal Magic

Tarot for Beginners: A Guide to Psychic Tarot Reading, Real Tarot Card Meanings, and Simple Tarot Spreads

Runes for Beginners: A Guide to Reading Runes in Divination, Rune Magic, and the Meaning of the Elder Futhark Runes

Wicca Moon Magic: A Wiccan's Guide and Grimoire for Working Magic with Lunar Energies

Wicca Wheel of the Year Magic: A Beginner's Guide to the Sabbats, with History, Symbolism, Celebration Ideas, and Dedicated Sabbat Spells

Wicca Kitchen Witchery: A Beginner's Guide to Magical Cooking, with Simple Spells and Recipes

Wicca Essential Oils Magic: A Beginner's Guide to Working with Magical Oils, with Simple Recipes and Spells

Wicca Elemental Magic: A Guide to the Elements, Witchcraft, and Magical Spells

Wicca Magical Deities: A Guide to the Wiccan God and Goddess, and Choosing a Deity to Work Magic With

Wicca Living a Magical Life: A Guide to Initiation and Navigating Your Journey in the Craft

Magic and the Law of Attraction: A Witch's Guide to the Magic of Intention, Raising Your Frequency, and Building Your Reality

Wicca Altar and Tools: A Beginner's Guide to Wiccan Altars, Tools for Spellwork, and Casting the Circle

Wicca Finding Your Path: A Beginner's Guide to Wiccan Traditions, Solitary Practitioners, Eclectic Witches, Covens, and Circles

Wicca Book of Shadows: A Beginner's Guide to Keeping Your Own Book of Shadows and the History of Grimoires

Modern Witchcraft and Magic for Beginners: A Guide to Traditional and Contemporary Paths, with Magical Techniques for the Beginner Witch

FREE GIFT REMINDER

As a thank-you gift to my readers, you can also download a free eBook version of *Wicca: Little Book of Spells.* These ten spells are ideal for newcomers to the practice of magic, but are also suitable for any level of experience!

You can download it by visiting:

<u>www.wiccaliving.com/bonus</u>

I hope you enjoy it!

DID YOU ENJOY
WICCA MOON MAGIC?

Thanks so much for reading this book! I know there are many great books out there about Wicca, so I really appreciate you choosing this one.

If you enjoyed the book, I have a small favor to ask—would you take a couple of minutes to leave a review for this book on Amazon?

Your feedback will help me to make improvements to this book, and to create even better ones in the future. It will also help me develop new ideas for books on other topics that might be of interest to you. Thanks in advance for your help!

Printed in Great Britain
by Amazon